THE RA MATERIAL

The Law of One
Book V

The Law of One
Book V

DON ELKINS   CARLA RUECKERT
JAMES ALLEN McCARTY

Copyright © 2020 by James Allen McCarty, Don Elkins, and Carla Rueckert
Library of Congress Control Number: 2020936710

First Printed 1998
ISBN: 978-0-924608-21-6

*3,000 copies of *The Law of One* were privately printed by L/L Research, Louisville, KY, before it was printed under the title *The Ra Material*.

All rights reserved. No part of this work may be reproduced or used in any form or by any means—graphic, electronic, or mechanical, including photocopying or information storage and retrieval systems—without written permission from the publisher.

The scanning, uploading, and distribution of this book or any part there of via the Internet or any other means without the permission of the publisher is illegal and punishable by law. Please purchase only authorized editions and do not participate in or encourage the electronic piracy of copyrighted materials.

"Red Feather Mind Body Spirit" logo is a trademark of Schiffer Publishing, Ltd.
"Red Feather Mind Body Spirit Feather" logo is a registered trademark of Schiffer Publishing, Ltd.

Type set in Chaparral Pro

Book V
Softcover ISBN: 978-0-924608-21-6
Hardcover ISBN: 978-0-7643-6558-4
Box Set ISBN (Books I–V): 978-0-7643-6021-3
E-Book ISBN: 978-1-5073-0119-7

Printed in India

Updated Edition
10 9 8 7 6 5 4 3 2

Published by Red Feather Mind, Body, Spirit
An imprint of Schiffer Publishing, Ltd.
4880 Lower Valley Road
Atglen, PA 19310
Phone: (610) 593-1777; Fax: (610) 593-2002
E-mail: Info@schifferbooks.com
Web: www.redfeathermbs.com

For our complete selection of fine books on this and related subjects, please visit our website at www.schifferbooks.com. You may also write for a free catalog.

Personal Material
Fragments Omitted from the First Four Books

with Commentary by
Jim McCarty and **Carla L. Rueckert**

  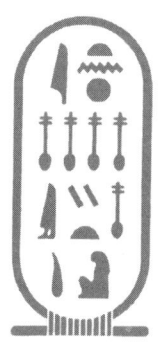 

CONTENTS

Introduction 9

The Fragments 11

Epilogue 193

Endnotes 197

Index 199

INTRODUCTION

[JIM] The material in this book was originally withheld from publication in the first four books of THE LAW OF ONE series because it is predominantly of a personal or sensitive nature, and it was our feeling that if this material were included, it would be easy for readers to become overly interested in the personalities behind this information, rather than focusing on the information itself. It is now our hope that we may be able to use this same information to illustrate the general application of this material to all seekers of truth. We are certain that this information has general application to people like you because we are people just like you, with the same range of human emotions, the same strengths and weaknesses, and the same desire to know what is loosely called the truth.

The death of Don Elkins, questioner for the Ra contact, in November 1984 marked the end of the Ra contact, because it was the harmony between the three of us that was the primary factor that allowed those of Ra to speak through our group. It is our opinion that in order to be of the most appropriate service, we must simply desire to serve without any conditions put on that desire. It was with that simple desire that we joined as a group at the end of 1980, and within three weeks we were amazed to be part of what developed into the Ra contact. We do not consciously seek a third person with whom to attempt to reestablish contact with those of Ra, because that would not be a full surrender of our will to the Greater Will and would be, rather, the imposition of our lesser and more distorted wills upon what is most appropriate for us as a way of being of service to others. It now feels like the appropriate time to share the last of the information that we have as a fruit of the contact with those of Ra with people who, like us, would like to read whatever Ra might have to say on any subject and use that speaking as catalyst for personal evolution.

Since the personal material comes from many of the 106 sessions that we completed during the Ra contact, it suffers from being quite disjointed. Through our written words we hope to be able to fashion a reasonably coherent fabric of our experiences into which each of the personal segments of the Ra contact may fit. Even the best of what we may write and share with you is mere human opinion. We are quite fallible and do not wish to place any stumbling block in your path, so please disregard any words that do not sound right to you. Use only those that ring true.

[**CARLA**] *Jim has taken the task of describing to you the circumstances in which each fragment was collected. My part is to add my viewpoint on many subjects, but perhaps most importantly on Don and me, which Jim has no way to address, as he did not know either of us until just three years before the contact with those of Ra. I echo Jim's feeling that it is time for the final bits of this contact to be shared. Those who have enjoyed Ra's thoughts will continue to appreciate the bon mots they are so good at giving us. We at L/L can sigh with relief now and say, yes, this is ALL of the material. There ain't no more! And without a doubt, the reader will see from these bits of our lives that we are just as foolish as the rest of humankind and are not to be confused with the source of these channelings. This I have come to count as a valuable thing.*

It has been the greatest privilege and the greatest challenge of my life to have had the care and feeding of Donald Tully Elkins for the last 16 years of his life. Never have two people loved more deeply, yet Don's need to remain aloof was such that none of his feelings were ever displayed to me, and this was my catalyst to work with. I treasured and cherished this dear man the very best I knew how, and honor him as the only truly great man I have ever personally met. It was his driving intellect that first posed the questions that the Ra contact attempted to answer. It was he who had the vision of living as a spiritual family rather than a nuclear one. Jim and I are very fortunate to have had such a man as our leader and ofttimes our teacher. And I have been blessed with a pure and faithful romance with a soulmate who means all to me. As you enjoy this last part of a contact that will likely never come again, just rejoice that Don Elkins lived and served among us wanderers with such devotion and light.

―― THE FRAGMENTS ――

Fragment 1

The beginning of Session 1 appears here precisely as it was received. In our first private printing of Book I of *The Law of One* we omitted a portion of this first session because Don felt that compared with the other twenty-five sessions of Book I, it was anomalistic—and perhaps too confusing as such—for first-time readers. That omission was reproduced when the mass market edition was printed by the Donning Company under the title of *The Ra Material*.

This is the only session in which Ra delivered anything close to what Brad Steiger has called a "cosmic sermonette" before beginning with the question-and-answer format that was used exclusively throughout the remainder of the Ra contact. Ra preferred the question-and-answer format because it allowed our free will to decide what information we would seek rather than their determining that choice for us by using the lecture method of teach/learning.

And it was interesting to us that Ra mentioned in this first session that they were not able to offer any "conditioning" to any instrument due to their own transmitting limitations. This conditioning often involves seemingly involuntary movement of some part of the vocal cords, mouth, lip, jaw, or some other physiological sensation that the one serving as instrument identifies with the approach of the contact. This session also marks the last time that Ra ever attempted to speak through any instrument other than Carla.

Since the channeling phenomenon has become so commonplace, we would like to make an additional comment on the conditioning vibration. Many who serve as instruments feel that they recognize the entities who speak through them by the conditioning vibration, and need no other identification to be sure that they are channeling whom they think they are channeling. We have found that this is not always so, because negative entities of the same relative vibration will feel just like the familiar positive entity to the one serving as instrument when the negative entity wishes to call itself by another name and mimic the positive entity as a part of the process of tricking the instrument and then detuning the positive work done by the group receiving its information. This is standard procedure for those of the path of service to self. The fundamental concept involved is that the opportunity for positive entities to speak through instruments and groups must be balanced by the same opportunity being offered to negative entities. This need not be a difficulty for any instrument, however, if it and its support group utilize the twin processes of tuning the group and challenging the contact each time channeling occurs.

Tuning the group is the process whereby each individual in the group refines the desire to serve others and puts it first and foremost in the mind and heart. The group may accomplish this tuning by any method that has meaning to each within the group, whether that be by singing sacred songs, chanting, praying, telling jokes, sharing information, visualizing light surrounding the group, or whatever blends each present into one unified source of seeking.

Then, when the instrument feels the entities that wish to channel through it are present, the challenge is mentally given, again in whatever way that feels appropriate to the instrument and in whatever way that the instrument can get behind with every fiber of its being. The instrument will demand to know if the entities wishing to channel through it come in the name of whatever principle the instrument feels is the highest and best in its own life. One may challenge the entity wishing to speak in the name of Jesus the Christ, the Christ consciousness, the positive polarity, service to others, or in the name of one of the archangels or in whatever represents the center of one's life, that for which the instrument lives and would gladly die. This forms a wall of light through which an entity of negative polarity has as much trouble passing through as you and I would discover with a solid brick wall.

Negative entities stand ready to fill in any lapse of care in this regard with their offering of service in their own way. They mimic the positive contact only as much as necessary to maintain the channel and then give false information whenever possible, usually having to do with dates and descriptions of upcoming cataclysmic earth changes, which, when made public by the group receiving such information, makes the group lose credibility since the dates are never correct. Thus the negative entity takes the spiritual strength of the light that the group had been able to share in service-to-others work.

Carla used this method of challenging Ra for the first two sessions. This was and is her normal method, as she usually does conscious channeling. But in the Ra contact she involuntarily went into trance and could not tune in that way, so we were glad when, at the end of the second session, Ra gave us the ritual of walking the Circle of One to replace the challenging procedure used in telepathic channeling, since in all sessions after the first two, Carla was immediately in the trance state, out of her body, and unaware of any activity whatsoever. None of us ever discovered how she was able to accomplish this trance state and the leaving of her body. It was apparently a pre-incarnatively chosen ability to aid in the contact with Ra. Our meditation before each session was our group process of tuning.

We used what Don called "tuned trance telepathy" to communicate with those of Ra. This is to say that while the contact was ongoing, neither Carla nor those of Ra inhabited Carla's body. Carla's spirit was apparently in the care of those of Ra while Ra used Carla's body from a distance to form the words that responded to Don's questions. Ra mentioned many times that they had only the grossest control over her body and had difficulty, for example, in repositioning her hands when one of them was experiencing pain flares due to her arthritic condition. Carla could not feel these pain flares, but repositioning them was sometimes necessary since the pain was like static on the line. This occurred only occasionally and was always noted in the text.

Don and Carla had been working together for twelve years, channeling, researching, and writing two books in the area of metaphysics before I joined them in December 1980. Unsure of what to do as the first project together, we considered rewriting one of those books, *Secrets of the UFO*, and I had begun background reading and taking notes. Three weeks later the first Ra contact occurred and was totally unexpected. It happened when Carla was conducting a teaching session in which one of the Sunday meditation group members was learning how to channel. Don sat in on the session, but I was out shopping and happened to walk in through the front door loaded with sacks of groceries just as Don was asking about the earth changes that were anticipated at the end of this cycle of growth. At that point Ra requested a moment to deepen Carla's trance state before continuing. Such an interruption never happened again, because after the second session we prepared another room especially for the Ra contact and continued to use the living room for all other meditations and teaching sessions. This first session is one of only four of the total 106 sessions with Ra in which anyone besides Don, Carla, and I attended. Since the three of us lived together, the harmony that we developed between us was very stable and was a critical ingredient in establishing and maintaining the contact.

These days, I am teaching very few people to channel. Through the years, I have seen the kind of havoc that an opened and untuned channel can wreak in the personality of the seeker who channels just for a while, or just for the fun of it. The basic problem with channeling tends to be that the channel needs to be actively attempting to live the message she is receiving. In spiritual work, no one has the luxury of saying, "Do as I say, not as I do." If we do not embody the principles we offer to others, we receive often-dramatic and life-shaking catalyst that points up the divergence of ideals from true intention. I have seen people lose their sanity when carelessly involved with channeling. So I take the responsibility of taking students very, very seriously. For the most part, I now work with people who come to me already channeling, and having difficulties with that. This has involved me with people being moved around the world by signals from Indians, UFO contactees with strange stories, and all manner of diverse folks who are in some way at risk in the "new age" sea of confusion. The phrase "spiritual counselor" has a smug, know-it-all feeling to it, which I hope I do not reflect, but it's pretty much what I am doing these days. Perhaps "spiritual listener" is more accurate. With email there has come a wider opportunity to relate with seekers personally. We welcome anyone's communication here at L/L Research and have never failed to answer any mail sent to us, so please feel free to address questions to us. We're delighted to help in any way we can. Our website address is www.llresearch.org; our email address is contact@llresearch.org.

Session 1,
January 15, 1981

RA: I am Ra. I have not spoken through this instrument before. We had to wait until she was precisely tuned as we send a narrow-band vibration. We greet you in the love and in the light of our Infinite Creator.

We have watched your group. We have been called to your group, for you have a need for the diversity of experiences in channeling which go with a more intensive or, as you might call it, advanced approach to the system of studying the pattern of illusions of your body, your mind, and your spirit, which you call seeking the truth. We hope to offer you a somewhat different slant upon the information which is always and ever the same.

The Confederation of Planets in the Service of the Infinite Creator has only one important statement. That statement, my friends, as you know, is that all things, all life, all of the creation is part of one original thought.

We will exercise each channel if we are able to. The reception of our beam is a somewhat more advanced feat than some of the more broad vibration channels opened by other members for more introductory and intermediate work.

Let us for a moment consider thought. What is it, my friends, to take thought? Took you then thought today? What thoughts did you think today? What thoughts were part of the original thought today? In how many of your thoughts did the creation lie? Was love contained? And was service freely given? You are not part of a material universe. You move your body, your mind, and your spirit in somewhat eccentric patterns, for you have not completely grasped the concept that you are part of the original thought.

We would at this time transfer to the instrument known as Don. I am Ra.

[pause]

RA: I am Ra. I am again with this instrument. We are close to initiating a contact, but we are having difficulty penetrating a certain mental tension and distraction that are somewhat characteristic of this channel. We will therefore describe the type of vibration which is being sent. The instrument will find us entering the energy field at a slight angle towards the back of the top of the head, in a narrow but strong area of intensity. We are not able to offer any conditioning due to our own transmitting limitations; therefore, if the instrument can feel this particular effect he may then speak our thoughts as they come to him. We will again attempt this contact. I am Ra.

[pause]

RA: This instrument is resisting our contact. However, we assure you that we are satisfied that contact with the one known as Don is not preferable to that instrument. We will, therefore, move on to the one known as Leonard. Again we caution the instrument that it is a narrow band of communication which is felt as a vibration entering the aura. We will now transfer this contact. I am Ra.

[pause]

RA: I am Ra. We greet you once more in the love and the light of our Infinite Creator. We ask that you be patient with us. We are a difficult channel to receive. We may perhaps add some dimensions to your understanding. At this time we would be glad to attempt to speak to any subject or question which those entities in the room may have potential use in the requesting.

Fragment 2

The following material in Session 6 concerns the basic requirement for the Ra contact; that is, harmony. During the 106 sessions with Ra, there were only three people who ever attended a Ra session besides the three of us, and in each case it was Ra's recommendation that each entity needed not only to have the appropriate attitude in its personal means of seeking, but that each person needed to be in harmony with each of us before attending any session. In Tom's case this was achieved by Don's explaining to Tom the meaning that the Bible, candle, incense, and chalice of water held for us as triggering mechanisms or signals to our subconscious minds that a session was about to take place, and that from all levels of our being we should begin the process of purifying our desires to serve others above all else and to surround ourselves with the joy-filled light of praise and thanksgiving. The harmony that this process produced among our group, then, was much as a musical chord with which those of Ra could blend their vibrations, and upon that harmonious blend of vibrations, information of a metaphysical nature could be transmitted by being drawn to those who sought it.

Tom is one of the members of L/L Research's spiritual family who attended our meditation group's Sunday meetings for some years. It is impossible to say how many "members" have come to our sessions over the years since 1962, when we began. Like many of these dear souls, he has kept in touch, although his personal path has taken him elsewhere. We have always attempted to "tune" our circle before we begin to meditate together, so Tom was perfectly clear on what we needed.

That altar, with its Christian accouterments, may well puzzle some who think that it takes a new-age channel to produce new-age information. Not so for me, unless one counts Jesus Christ as a new-age channel himself! I was a cradle Anglican and have attended Episcopal churches my whole life. That those of Ra worked with these deeply ingrained biases within me is, to me, a signal characteristic of this unique source. I felt loved, accepted, and cherished by having these items placed near me, and that they thought this out was a constant blessing during this contact.

Session 6,
January 24, 1981

QUESTIONER: I would like to ask if it is possible for Tom to attend one of these sessions tomorrow. Are you familiar with the entity Tom?

RA: I am Ra. This mind/body/spirit complex sound vibration "Tom" is acceptable. We caution you to instruct this entity in the frame of mind and various appurtenances which it must understand before it is conducted into the circle.

QUESTIONER: I'm not quite sure what you mean by appurtenances.

RA: I was referring to the symbolic objects which trigger this instrument's distortions towards love/light. The placement and loving acceptance of them by all present is important in the nurturing of this instrument. Therefore, the appurtenances involved must be described and their presence explained in your own words of teach/learning, for you have the proper attitude for the required results.

QUESTIONER: The only question that I have is that I will assume that since Leonard was here when you first made contact that it is suitable for him to be here as well as Tom.

RA: This is correct and completes the number of those at this time able to come who are suitable. Again, remember the instructions given for the preparation of the vibratory sound complex Tom.

Fragment 3

Early in the Ra contact we received answers to our questions that fell into a controversial portion of our third-density illusion. Almost everyone, at some point within the study of the paranormal, spends some time being fascinated by the so-called conspiracy theories, which have generally to do with the supposedly unseen groups and individuals who are said to be the real powers behind governments and their activities in the world today. Such theories usually hold that the news reports that we hear and read concerning politics, economics, the military, and so forth are but the tip of a very large iceberg that has mainly to do with various schemes for world domination and that functions through the secret activities of this small, elite group of human beings and their alien allies.

The following information falls into this category and resulted from a follow-up question Don asked about UFOs and their sources. You will note Don's incredulous attitude throughout this portion of his questioning. It was our decision to remove this information from Book I of *The Law of One* because we felt it to be entirely unimportant and of a transient nature, since knowing it adds nothing to one's ability or desire to seek the truth and the nature of the evolutionary process, whether the information is true or not. In fact, knowing and continuing to seek this kind of information can become a major stumbling block to one's spiritual journey because it removes one's attention from the eternal truths that may serve anyone's journey—at any time—and places it upon that which is only of fleeting interest and of little use spiritually. Concentrating on conspiracy theories and their participants tends to reinforce the illusion of separation and ignores the love that binds all things as One Being. If we had continued to pursue this particular line of questioning, or any other line of questioning of a transient nature, we would soon have lost the contact with those of Ra because, as Ra mentioned in the very first session, Ra communicated with us through a "narrow band" of vibration or wave length.

Through various clues that Ra gave us when Don asked about the alignments at the end of each session, we were able to determine that this "narrow band" meant that only information of the purest and most precise nature concerning the process of the evolution of mind, body, and spirit could be successfully transmitted on a sustainable basis through our instrument. To ask Ra questions of a transient nature would be like trying to run a finely tuned engine on crude petroleum.

Many groups become fascinated with transient information of a specific, mundane nature and have their information polluted by negative entities, who gradually replace the positive entities that began their contact. Pursuing information of this kind is like moving the dial on your radio so that you end up with another station altogether from the one with which you began. This change in desire for the kind of information that the group seeks from its contact is the signal to that contact that what it has to offer is no longer desired, and the Law of Free Will requires that only hints of this detuning process be given to the group so that all choices that the group makes are totally a product of its free will. When a group continues to seek the transient information, the positive contact gives hints here and there that such information is not of importance, but when the group persists in seeking this kind of information, the positive contact, in order to observe the free will of the group, must slowly withdraw and is then eventually replaced by a negative contact, which is only too happy to give this kind of information, but with less desire for accuracy and with maximal desire to remove the group from the ranks of those who serve others. When the group has been discredited by false information—such as dates of future disasters that are publicized by the group and then do not occur—then the negative entities have been successful in removing the power of the group's light and have gathered it for themselves.

We still feel that this information is totally unimportant, and the only reason that we include it now is to show how easy it is for a group to get off the track, shall we say, and to lose the focus of desire for that which is important and that with which the group began: the desire to serve others by gathering information that may aid in the evolution of mind, body, and spirit. Ten thousand years from now, it will not matter one whit who did what to whom on this tiny speck of whirling dust. All that will matter is that love may be found at any time in every person and particle of the one creation, or any illusion thereof. Hopefully information gained through any effort such as the Ra contact will help some other third-density entities to discover more of that truth and to move one step further on their evolutionary journey to the One Creator.

All I can add to this is a plea to all official sources: we do not know anything, we are not in on any conspiracies, and please, please don't tap our telephones ... again! When Don and I joined Andrija Puharich for a mind link in 1977, we caught the attention of some agency who played havoc with our telephone system. And how utterly without use to listen in to our converse! Mystics seldom plot! We honestly don't care about this stuff and just stumbled into it by accident.

I'd like to point out the way those of Ra seem here somewhat off-balance compared to their usual steady selves. It is subtle, but easy to see—the opening to each answer is normally "I am Ra." Several times in this fragment, however, that signature is missing. The contact was going slightly out of tune here, I think, due to the information's transient nature.

Session 8,
January 26, 1981

QUESTIONER: There was a portion of the material from yesterday that I will read where you say, "There is a certain amount of landing taking place. Some of these landings are of your own people; some are of the group known to you as Orion." My first question is, what did you mean that some of the landings are of your peoples?

RA: I am Ra. Your peoples have, at this time/space present, the technological achievement, if you would call it that, of being able to create and fly the shape and type of craft known to you as unidentified flying objects. Unfortunately for the social memory complex vibratory rate of your peoples, these devices are not intended for the service of mankind, but for potential destructive use. This further muddles the vibratory nexus of your social memory complex, causing a situation where neither those oriented towards serving others nor those oriented towards serving self can gain the energy/power which opens the gates to intelligent infinity for the social memory complex. This in turn causes the harvest to be small.

QUESTIONER: Are these craft that are from our peoples from what we call planes that are not incarnate at this time? Where are they based?

RA: I am Ra. These of which we spoke are of third density and are part of the so-called military complex of various of your peoples' societal divisions or structures.

The bases are varied. There are bases, as you would call them, undersea in your southern waters near the Bahamas, as well as in your Pacific seas in various places close to your Chilean borders on the water. There are bases upon your moon, as you call this satellite, which are at this time being reworked. There are bases which move about your lands. There are bases, if you would call them that, in your skies. These are the bases of your peoples, very numerous and, as we have said, potentially destructive.

QUESTIONER: Where do the people who operate these craft come from? Are they affiliated with any nation on Earth? What is their source?

RA: These people come from the same place as you or I. They come from the Creator.

As you intend the question, in its shallower aspect, these people are those in your and other selves' governments responsible for what you would term national security.

QUESTIONER: Am I to understand then that the United States has these craft in undersea bases?

RA: I am Ra. You are correct.

QUESTIONER: How did the United States learn the technology to build these craft?

RA: I am Ra. There was a mind/body/spirit complex known to your people by the vibratory sound complex Nikola. This entity departed the illusion, and the papers containing the necessary understandings were taken by mind/body/spirit complexes serving your security of national divisional complex. Thus your people became privy to the basic technology. In the case of those mind/body/spirit complexes which you call Russians, the technology was given from one of the Confederation in an attempt, approximately twenty-seven of your years ago, to share information and bring about peace among your peoples. The entities giving this information were in error, but we did many things at the end of this cycle in attempts to aid your harvest, from which we learned the folly of certain types of aid. That is a contributing factor to our more cautious approach at this date, even as the need is power upon power greater, and your peoples' call is greater and greater.

QUESTIONER: I'm puzzled by these craft which have undersea bases. Is this technology sufficient to overshadow all other armaments? Do we have the ability to just fly in these craft, or are they just craft for transport? What is the basic mechanism of their power source? It's really hard to believe is what I'm saying.

RA: I am Ra. The craft are perhaps misnamed in some instances. It would be more appropriate to consider them as weaponry. The energy used is that of the field of electromagnetic energy which polarizes the Earth sphere. The weaponry is of two basic kinds: that which is called by your peoples psychotronic and that which is called by your peoples particle beam. The amount of destruction which is contained in this technology is considerable, and the weapons have been used in many cases to alter weather patterns and to enhance the vibratory change which engulfs your planet at this time.

QUESTIONER: How have they been able to keep this a secret? Why aren't these craft in use for transport?

RA: The governments of each of your societal-division illusions desire to refrain from publicity so that the surprise may be retained in case of hostile action from what your peoples call enemies.

QUESTIONER: How many of these craft does the United States have?

RA: I am Ra. The United States has 573 at this time. They are in the process of adding to this number.

QUESTIONER: What is the maximum speed of one of these craft?

RA: I am Ra. The maximum speed of these craft is equal to the Earth energy squared. This field varies. The limit is approximately one-half the light speed, as you would call it. This is due to imperfections in design.

QUESTIONER: Would this type of craft come close to solving many of the energy problems as far as transport goes?

RA: I am Ra. The technology your peoples possess at this time is capable of resolving each and every limitation which plagues your social memory complex at this present nexus of experience. However, the concerns of some of your beings with distortions towards what you would call powerful energy cause these solutions to be withheld until the solutions are so needed that those with the distortion can then become further distorted in the direction of power.

QUESTIONER: You also said that some of the landings at this time were of the Orion group. Why did the Orion group land here? What is their purpose?

RA: I am Ra. Their purpose is conquest, unlike those of the Confederation who wait for the calling. The so-called Orion group calls itself to conquest.

QUESTIONER: Specifically, what do they do when they land?

RA: There are two types of landings. In the first, entities among your peoples are taken on their craft and programmed for future use. There are two or three levels of programming. First, the level that will be discovered by those who do research. Second, a triggering program. Third, a second and most deep triggering program crystallizing the entity, thereby rendering it lifeless and useful as a kind of beacon. This is a form of landing.

The second form is that of landing beneath the Earth's crust, which is entered from water. Again, in the general area of your South American and Caribbean areas and close to the so-called northern pole. The bases of these people are underground.

QUESTIONER: The most startling information that you have given me, which I must admit that I'm having difficulty believing, is that the United States has 573 craft of the type which you described. How many people of United States designation are aware of these craft, including those who operate them?

RA: I am Ra. The number of your peoples varies, for there are needs to communicate at this particular time/space nexus so that the number is expanding at this time. The approximate number is 1,500. It is only approximate, for as your illusory time/space continuum moves from present to present at this nexus, many are learning.

QUESTIONER: Where are these craft constructed?

RA: These craft are constructed one by one in two locations: in the desert or arid regions of your so-called New Mexico and in the desert or arid regions of your so-called Mexico, both installations being under the ground.

QUESTIONER: Am I to believe that the United States actually has a manufacturing plant in Mexico?

RA: I am Ra. I spoke thusly. May I, at this time, reiterate that this type of information is very shallow and of no particular consequence compared to the study of the Law of One. However, we carefully watch these developments in hopes that your peoples are able to be harvested in peace.

QUESTIONER: I am totally aware that this line of questioning is of totally no consequence at all, but this particular information is so startling to me that it makes me question your validity on this. Up until this point I was in agreement with everything you had said. This is very startling to me. It just does not seem possible to me that this secret could have been kept for twenty-seven years, and that we are operating these craft. I apologize for my attitude, but I thought that I would be very honest. It is unbelievable to me that we would operate a plant in Mexico, outside of the United States, to build these craft. Maybe I'm mistaken. These craft are physical craft built by physical people? Could I go get in one and ride in one? Is that correct?

RA: I am Ra. This is incorrect. You could not ride one. The United States, as you call your society divisional complex, creates these as a type of weapon.

QUESTIONER: There are no occupants then? No pilot, shall I say?

RA: I am Ra. This is correct.

QUESTIONER: How are they controlled?

RA: I am Ra. They are controlled by computer from a remote source of data.

QUESTIONER: Why do we have a plant in Mexico?

RA: I am Ra. The necessity is both for dryness of the ground and for a near-total lack of population. Therefore, your so-called government and the so-called government of your neighboring geographical vicinity arranged for an underground installation. The government officials who agreed did not know the use to which their land would be put, but thought it a governmental research installation for use in what you would call bacteriological warfare.

QUESTIONER: Is this the type of craft that Dan Frye was transported in?

RA: I am Ra. The one known as Daniel was, in thought-form, transported by Confederation thought-form vehicular illusion in order to give this mind/body/spirit complex data so that we might see how this type of contact aided your people in the uncovering of the intelligent infinity behind the illusion of limits.

QUESTIONER: The reason that I have questioned you so much and so carefully about the craft which you say the United States government operates is that if we include this in the book, it will create numerous problems. It is something that I am considering leaving out of the book entirely, or I am going to have to question you in considerable detail about it. It's difficult to even question in this area, but I would like to ask a few more questions about it, with the possible option of leaving it in the book. What is the diameter of the craft which the United States has?

RA: I am Ra. I suggest that this be the last question for this session. We will speak as you deem fit in further sessions, asking you to be guided by your own discernment only.
    The approximate diameter, given several model changes, is 23 of your feet, as you measure.

Fragment 4
None of us were ever greatly interested in previous incarnational experiences. Again, it's easy to lose the focus on the present moment's opportunities for growth if one becomes overly interested in one's lives before this one. The one query of this nature that we did ask of Ra elicited an answer that seemed to support our lack of interest in past lives.

I do personally believe that we incarnate many times, and that we fashion, through these cycles of manifestation, complex and meaningful relationships that root deeply within our beings. When Don and I met, he has said he knew for certain that we would be together. Since what immediately thereafter ensued for me was a four-year marriage to a fellow who wished not to be married, I once braced him for not having told me this home truth right then in 1962, and saved me that difficult four years. "What? And have you miss all that good catalyst?" he said.

Both Donald and Jim had a loving and generous regard of me that is amazing unless one introduces the concept of previous connections. I have no doubt that we have served together before, in other lives and other times. An interesting bit of possible past history was expressed years ago to Jim in a psychic reading: it was suggested that in the American great plains frontier of the nineteenth century, Don and Jim were brothers living together as farmers. I was Jim's child, Don's nephew, and I lived only to the age of five, being sickly from birth. This was suggested as being preparation for their taking care of me in this life, as I dealt with disability, limitation, and especially psychic greeting during the time of the Ra contact. It rings true at some level with me. However, I also feel that we do not need to know anything of our past associations in order to learn and serve together at this present moment. We have all we need to meet the present moment. The rest is just details.

Session 9,
January 27, 1981

QUESTIONER: Is it possible for you to tell us anything about our past experiences, our past incarnations before this incarnation?

RA: I am Ra. It is possible. However, such information as this is carefully guarded by your mind/body/spirit being totality so that your present space/time experiences will be undiluted.

Let us scan for harmless material for your beingness. I am, in the distortion of desire for your freedom from preconception, able to speak only generally. There have been several times when this group worked and dwelt together. The relationships varied. There is balanced karma, as you call it; each thus teacher of each. The work has involved healing, understanding the uses of the earth energy, and work in aid of civilizations which called just as your sphere has done and we have come. This ends the material which we consider harmless.

Fragment 5
In the first paragraph of the next section, one can see how easy it is for even the most serious of seekers occasionally to lose the proper

attitude for finding the heart of the evolutionary process. Properly attuning one's being for efficient seeking has far less to do with what one does than with how one does it and how one balances it or seats it within one's being with meditation and contemplation. Without the balance of the meditative attitude, the mind tends to become distracted by the mundane repetition of events, and one's lessons tend to orbit the periphery of one's being without becoming seated in the center of the being, there to provide a deeper grasp of the nature of this illusion and a sense of how to navigate one's self through it in a more harmonious fashion. We also see in Ra's next response that it is imperative that all such navigational movements of one's being be a product of one's free will choices, never to be abridged by any other being. That point is echoed again in Ra's response to Don's query about the metaphysical implications of attempting to lock a Man in Black in one's closet, an opportunity that we never had, incidentally!

This is another good example of a line of questioning veering off into transient and unimportant information. Note how Ra ends Session 12 in Book I, also titled *The Ra Material*, with hints that the "correct alignment" and "proper orientation" of the Bible, candle, censer, and water are somewhat askew. It took us twelve sessions to determine that Ra was not actually speaking of the physical placement of the Bible and so forth, but Ra was giving us a hint that our metaphysical alignment was off. Our line of questioning was misplaced from the heart of the evolutionary process. Since our contact with Ra was "narrow band," that meant that Ra could not long respond to questions that were off the target. If we had allowed these distortions to remain over a long period of time, the contact would have been impaired and eventually we would have lost the contact.

The last portion of this session deals with the concept of what is called the Wanderers, and their frequently shared characteristics of exhibiting physical ailments such as allergies and personality disorders, which, in the deeper sense, seem to be a reaction against this planet's vibrational frequency. This is apparently a side effect that is due to such entities having another planetary influence in a higher density as their home vibration. They incarnate on this third-density planet in order to be of service in whatever way is possible to help the population of this planet to become more aware of the evolutionary process and to move in harmony with it. These Wanderers go through the same forgetting process that every other third-density being who incarnates here goes through, and they become completely the third-density being—even as they slowly begin to remember why it is that they have been born here. Apparently, about one in every seventy people on Earth is of such an origin.

It almost seems to be in vogue now to say that one is from this or that planet, this or that higher density, and that one is really this or that exalted being come down to Earth to be a great teacher. It is embarrassing to us to see such a magnificent opportunity for rendering a humble service cheapened to a game of who has the most spiritual sergeant's stripes. We do not hide the possibility that we may be of such origins, but neither do we nor those of Ra feel that such an origin is particularly remarkable. As Don used to say, "You've got to be somewhere doing something. You might as well be here doing this."

I think one thing to keep in mind, if we are Wanderers from elsewhere, is that we came here for a reason: to serve at this time right here in this very shadow world of Earth's third density. Yes, we suffer the results of trying to live in a vibratory range that is difficult for us, and yes, we somehow remember a "better way" to live. With this in mind, it becomes clearer that our main mission here is simply to live, to breathe the air, and to let the love within us flow. Just the simple living of an everyday life is sacramental when the person is living with that consciousness of "all is love" humming its tune beneath our words and thoughts. To live devotionally does not mean, necessarily, that one becomes a hermit or a wandering pilgrim, although if you feel called to it, blessings on your way. To me, at least, the daily things are the most holy: the washing up, the chores, the errands. All moves in rhythm, and we are just part of that symphony of all life that shares energy back and forth.

I know that one of the great hopes a Wanderer has is to find its service. The living of a devotional life, right in the busy midst of everything, is ample and perfect service. It is what we came here to do. As we let love flow through us, others change, and as they open their hearts, the circle of light grows. We are now at a stage where the light sources are beginning to connect . . . do I hear the sound of global mind being born?

The global mind is a very real concept to me, as well, especially since the advent of email and the World Wide Web. With information being exchanged without pen or paper, we are basically working with light, surely one of the purer ways to communicate. As I collect stories of Wanderers' blues, I am struck by how intense and constant is the general desire for a spiritual home, an identity, and a way of service. I encourage all those who experience themselves as Wanderers to link up and "network" with other awakened consciousnesses, to live in the open heart together and allow the light to come through us all into the "world-wide web" of planetary consciousness. As Jim says, there is no greater service than being yourself in this sometimes refractory world.

Don loved Andrija Puharich and was a loyal and generous friend to him for many years. We met Andrija in 1974, after we read the book URI, which he wrote, and identified him as one of the characters in our oddly prophetic novel, The Crucifixion of Esmerelda Sweetwater, *which we had written in 1968 and 1969. We helped with the now-historic "Mind Link" of 1977 and heard from him from far and wide as he dodged bullets and various agents of various governments who thought he was up to something. Puharich was a person of immense hospitality and kindness of character, although quite insensitive to and unaware of the world and its requirements outside his work. This was a guy who got up in the morning and worked steadily, only stopping to grab some food, literally, until time for bed. He rather ran through people, using their talents and donations as they aided the work, and unaware of depleting people's resources or time, because he focused on the work before him, never on making money. This was a born scholar and a brilliant man, and much occurred in his ken. It is a loss to the world of ideas that his carefully kept journals were confiscated at the time of his death and have disappeared. I admit readily to feeling ofttimes that he was "using" Don. I felt he was a man of more energy, but less wisdom, than Don. I felt he should have followed Don's sage council at times. Don himself never felt anything like this. He was glad to help. I celebrate Andrija. What a singular and remarkable fellow, and what a contribution he made in so many ways!*

George Hunt Williamson was a channel we greatly admired; indeed, we used his channeling of Brother Philip in our tape Messages from the UFOs. *We were in telephone contact with him only, and like Andrija, he never made it to our sessions. It's likely he was not too pleased at Ra's request for him to prepare! He is one of the great pioneers in UFO and related metaphysical research, and I think the first to name Wanderers. He called them "apples," quoting the radio-channeled UFO message "To the apples we salt, we shall return."*

Session 12,
January 28, 1981

QUESTIONER: I got a call from Henry Puharich this afternoon, and he will be here next month. I would like to ask if it is permissible for him to join in our circle and ask questions. I would also like to ask if Michel D'Obrenovic, also known as George Hunt Williamson, could join our circle as well.

RA: I am Ra. These entities, at present, are not properly attuned for the particular work due to vibrational distortions, which in turn are due to a recent lack of time/space which you call busyness. It would be requested that the entities spend a brief time/space in each diurnal cycle of your planet in contemplation. At a future time/space in your continuum, you are requested to ask again. This group is highly balanced to this instrument's vibratory distortions due to, firstly, contact with the instrument on a day-to-day basis. Secondly, due to contact with the instrument through meditation periods. Thirdly, through a personal mind/body/spirit complex distortion towards contemplation, which in sum causes this group to be effective.

QUESTIONER: Which group was it that contacted Henry Puharich in Israel around 1972?

RA: I am Ra. We must refrain from answering this query due to the possibility/probability that the one you call Henry will read this answer. This would cause distortions in his future. It is necessary that each being use free and complete discernment from within the all-self which is at the heart of the mind/body/spirit complex.

QUESTIONER: Would that also keep you from answering who it was that the group I was in, in 1962, contacted then?

RA: I am Ra. This query may be answered. The group contacted was the Confederation.

QUESTIONER: Did they have any of their craft in our area at that time?

RA: I am Ra. There was no craft. There was a thought-form.

QUESTIONER: If a Man In Black were to visit me and I locked him in the closet, could I keep him, or would he disappear?

RA: I am Ra. It depends upon which type of entity you grab. You are perhaps able to perceive a construct. The construct might be kept for a brief period, although these constructs also have an ability to disappear. The programming on these constructs, however, makes it more difficult to remotely control them. You would not be able to grapple with a thought-form entity of the Man in Black, as you call it, type.

QUESTIONER: Would this be against the Law of One? Would I be making a mistake by grabbing one of those entities?

RA: I am Ra. There are no mistakes under the Law of One.

QUESTIONER: What I mean to ask is, would I be polarizing more towards self-service or service to others when I did this act of locking up the thought-form or construct?

RA: I am Ra. You may consider that question for yourself. We interpret the Law of One, but not to the extent of advice.

QUESTIONER: Is there a way for these Wanderers to heal themselves of their physical ailments?

RA: I am Ra. This will be the last complete question of this time/space.
The self-healing distortion is effected through realization of the intelligent infinity resting within. This is blocked in some way in these who are not perfectly balanced in bodily complexes. The blockage varies from entity to entity. It requires the conscious awareness of the spiritual nature of reality, if you will, and the corresponding pourings of this reality into the individual mind/body/spirit complex for healing to take place.
Is there a short question before we close this session?

QUESTIONER: Is it possible for you to tell us if any of the three of us are Wanderers?

RA: I am Ra. In scanning each of the mind/body/spirit complexes present, we find an already complete sureness of this occurrence and, therefore, find no harm in recapitulating this occurrence. Each of those present are [sic] Wanderers pursuing a mission, if you will.

Fragment 6
However, our curiosity did periodically return. And, once again, we see the importance of maintaining one's free will by not diluting the present incarnational experience with too much information concerning one's previous experiences. Meditations and lives tend to be more efficient if they remain focused upon one point or moment.

We have spent a few moments of our lives thinking about who was fifth density and who was sixth, but it has never been clear, nor have we been much pushed to figure it out!

Session 15,
January 30, 1981

QUESTIONER: Is it possible, since we are Wanderers, for you to tell us anything about which our last density was, which density we came from?

RA: I scan each and find it acceptable to share this information. The Wanderers in this working are of two densities: one the density of five; that is, of light; one the density of love/light, or unity. To express the identity of which came from which density, we observe this to be an infringement upon the free will of each. Therefore, we state simply the two densities, both of which are harmoniously oriented towards work together.

Fragment 7

The following material on "silver flecks" is curious in that these small, shiny pieces of what looked like silver rectangles would occasionally appear on or around us when we were discussing matters of a metaphysical nature. Apparently, if we were on the track of thinking that was felt appropriate by our subconscious minds, we would be given a sign of this correctness in the form of the "silver fleck." There are apparently many, many different ways in which people may receive such subconscious confirmations of the appropriateness of their thoughts or actions. The most common, of course, is that feeling of rightness that wells up from within when one is on the right track or receiving spiritually helpful information.

The awareness of this method of feedback from the winds of destiny is most helpful to one on a spiritual path. The natural world seems very open to the production of synchronicities that are subjectively meaningful. Once the seeker "gets" the presence of these signs and begins consciously to watch for them, she can actually have influence in the creating of more-subjective signs, until there are times when meaningful coincidence seems to take on a constant presence in her life. I certainly have found these signs most comforting and strengthening.

Session 16,
January 31, 1981

QUESTIONER: Can you tell me of the silver flecks that we have found sometimes on our faces or elsewhere?

RA: I am Ra. These of which you speak are a materialization of a subjectively oriented signpost indicating to one mind/body/spirit complex, and no other, a meaning of subjective nature.

QUESTIONER: Who creates these silver flecks?

RA: I am Ra. Picture, if you will, the increasing potential for learn/teaching. At some point a sign will be given indicating the appropriateness or importance of that learn/teaching. The entity itself, in cooperation with the inner planes, creates whatever signpost is most understandable or noticeable to it.

QUESTIONER: I understand then that we ourselves create this?

RA: I am Ra. Entities consciously do not create these. The roots of mind complex, having touched in understanding, intelligent infinity, create them.

Fragment 8

Before each contact with those of Ra, we conducted a meditation that we used as our tuning device; that is, our means of becoming as one in our seeking to be of service to others. Oftentimes during this meditation, Don would get a hunch as to an addition to the line of questioning that we had decided upon the night before. In Session 17, such a hunch came to him concerning a crater in the Tunguska region of Russia, which, it is speculated, was made by either a crashed UFO or a large meteor of some kind in 1908. There is also speculation that some scientists of the Soviet Union first became interested in the possibility of life in other parts of the galaxy and solar system as a result of their investigation of this crater and its possible origin.

After asking about this crater and following it up with questions concerning the development of nuclear energy on Earth, and the odd and rarely reported phenomenon of spontaneous combustion of a human being, Don determined that this line of questioning would yield little of value.

Donald was a scientist, and he never could quite accept that Ra was in no position to chat with us about phenomena that can be measured. The desire that had brought Ra to our group was a true desire for nontransient material, and this desire fueled our sessions. When we departed from that level of information, Ra would remind us to get back on track in a subtle way: by telling us to watch our alignments. We at first took them literally and thought they were referring to the items on the altar, to getting them lined up rightly. Later, we figured out that they were grading our questions, not our Bible and candle placement. It's worth emphasizing that anything measurable is also transient. The human spirit, the force of creative love, the creation's essence: these things are unfindable, noumenal, always sensed, and never penetrated by our fact-finding intellects. But we sense into them through living with an open heart, and by talking about them with sources such as Ra and Q'uo and other "universal" or "outer" energies and essences. The personal guides and other teachers of the inner planes of our planet have much more leeway in offering personal information, whenever their last incarnation. Go to them to get your readings on your health and other specific issues. Go to outer sources such as our confederation sources with questions that transcend space and time. If it will matter less in 10,000 years than it does now, it is probably not a universal question!

Session 17,
February 3, 1981

QUESTIONER: In meditation I got the question about the crater in Russia in the, I believe, Tunguska region. Can you tell me what caused the crater?

RA: I am Ra. The destruction of a fission reactor caused this crater.

QUESTIONER: Whose reactor?

RA: I am Ra. This was what you may call a "drone" sent by Confederation, which malfunctioned. It was moved to an area where its destruction would not cause infringement upon the will of mind/body/spirit complexes. It was then detonated.

QUESTIONER: What was its purpose in coming here?

RA: It was a drone designed to listen to the various signals of your peoples. You were, at that time, beginning work in a more technical sphere. We were interested in determining the extent and the rapidity of your advances. This drone was powered by a simple fission motor or engine, as you would call it. It was not that type which you now know, but was very small. However, it has the same destructive effect upon third-density molecular structures. Thus, as it malfunctioned, we felt it was best to pick a place for its destruction rather than attempt to retrieve it, for the possibility/probability modes for this maneuver looked very, very minute.

QUESTIONER: Was its danger both blast and radiation?

RA: I am Ra. There is very little radiation, as you know of it, in this particular type of device. There is radiation which is localized, but the localization is such that it does not drift with the winds as does the emission of your somewhat primitive weapons.

QUESTIONER: I believe that analysis has detected very little radiation in the trees in this area. Is this low level of radiation a result of what you are speaking of?

RA: I am Ra. This is correct. The amount of radiation is very localized. However, the energy which is released is powerful enough to cause difficulties.

QUESTIONER: Then was the Confederation responsible for the Earth receiving nuclear power?

RA: I am Ra. It is a point which one cannot judge what is cause. The basic equation which preceded this work was an equation brought through by a Wanderer dedicated to service to the planet. That this work should have become the foundation for instruments of destruction was not intended and was not given.

QUESTIONER: Can you tell me who this Wanderer was who brought through the equation?

RA: I am Ra. This information seems harmless, as this entity is no longer of your planetary third density. This entity was named sound vibratory complex Albert.

QUESTIONER: Is this the reason for what we call spontaneous combustion of human beings?

RA: I am Ra. This is not correct.

QUESTIONER: Can you tell me what causes that phenomenon?

RA: I am Ra. Picture, if you will, a forest. One tree is struck by lightning. It burns. Lightning does not strike elsewhere. Elsewhere does not burn. There are random occurrences which do not have to do with the entity, but with the window phenomenon of which we spoke.

QUESTIONER: Are these entities uniquely the same, or are they random entities?

RA: I am Ra. The latter is correct.

Fragment 9

At the beginning of Session 18, in response to a general query from Don concerning the information Ra was transmitting to our group, Ra innocently "told on" Carla. A good friend of hers had offered her the opportunity to experience the effects of LSD, which she had never experienced before. She used it twice in early February 1981 as a programming device to attempt to achieve an experience of unity with the Creator, but she did not wish Don to know about these experiences, since he was very much against the use of any illegal substances at any time and especially during the time during which our group was working with the Ra contact. In a later session it will be suggested by Ra that these two experiences were arranged by the negative entities monitoring our work with those of Ra, in hopes that Carla's ability to serve in the Ra contact might be hindered. As a result of this particular session, it was the determination of the three of us that there would be no further use of any illegal substances for as long as we were privileged to work with the Ra contact, so that no chinks in our "armor of light" that we could eliminate would be present, and so that the Ra contact could never be associated with the use of any such drugs.

The information on Aleister Crowley is self-explanatory and underlines again the caution that each seeker must take in moving carefully through its energy centers in a balanced fashion.

By chance, a few sessions earlier, we had discovered that sexual intercourse was an aid to Carla's vital energies during the trance state and would increase the length of a session if engaged in the night before a session was to be held. Thus, at the end of Session 18, when Don asked how we might avoid further difficulties in the contact, Ra affirmed the aid that we had discovered sexual intercourse provided. We also found that the conscious dedication of the act of love-making to the service of others via the Ra contact increased its beneficial effects.

As a young college woman, I never dated or spent time with anyone who smoked marijuana or took LSD, or any other drugs. People all around me were experimenting, but I never was offered any drugs. It was the day of flower children and high ideals, a wonderful time to be young. The hippies ruled, but I was only an honorary flower child, since I worked steadily throughout that decade. In 1981, I was thirty-eight. When an old friend offered to let me try LSD, I was tickled and eager to try it, for I had long been curious to see what this much-touted substance did to one's head. In the event, I thoroughly enjoyed the experiences—I tried LSD twice—and found that there really was a wonderful increase in the sense of rightness of things under its benign influence on me. Since then, I have heard from many people that my utterly positive experiences with LSD were somewhat atypical, in that most people deal with at least a little hallucination or departure from consensus reality, or even a negatively experienced "high" or bad trip. So I was either lucky or my subconscious mind was more settled in its own skin than some others. I'd bet on luck!

Needless to say, I was not happy to learn that Ra had blithely told my secret to Don. I valued Don's opinion above all things, and he was not pleased with my judgment in taking illegal substances. But I did not, and do not, feel guilty or ashamed for satisfying my curiosity under circumstances as safe as one could make them. I also have tried cigarettes and alcohol, both heavily addictive substances, but rarely drink and never use tobacco. (In cooking, however, I use many different spirits, as they offer such delightful notes when put into the harmony of cooking things.) My curiosity was satisfied and I moved on. The freedom to do this, to know what is out there, is a valuable one, to my mind, if not abused. Moderation seems to me the key.

I have very fond memories of reading Aleister Crowley's autohagiography to Don. He did not like to read, so I frequently read to him. Once we got into this outrageous, brilliant man's work, we were fascinated. Crowley is a fine writer, regardless of what his polarity might have been fumbling around with. Our favorite poem of his is a perfectly ghoulish nursery rhyme he wrote as a precocious toddler. It begins, "In her hospital bed she lay, rotting away, rotting away, rotting by night and rotting by day, rotting and rotting and rotting away." Now that I have told you this, you may perhaps see why this character grew up to become . . . eccentric! But always interesting.

In working to fit myself into Don's requirements for a mate, I became a user of relative ethics, a practice that seems always to offer a challenge eventually. Don wished to be celibate, which became obvious to me within six months of our coming together in 1968. I always said that his inability to resist me for those first few months we lived together was my greatest compliment of all time! I attempted a celibate life, after we had talked this issue through, for a little over two years, before I concluded that celibacy was not for me. Don had also decided that we should not marry. This implied, to me, a relationship based on a commonality in a metaphysical rather than a physical sense. Always logical, I suggested to Don that we make an agreement: I would tell him before I took a lover and when I had ceased seeing him. In between, there was no need to discuss it. This would preclude his hearing about such company from others. As he was gone flying about half the time, I had no difficulty in finding time for the lovers' relationship. My lover for most of the time Don and I spent together, ten of the sixteen years, was a trusted and much-loved buddy of mine ever since high school. We had thought of marriage years before and then decided against it, but we'd remained close. He got the notion to come see me perhaps once a month. I stopped seeing him when he began to wish to take our relationship further, and I was celibate again for some four years before Jim. When Jim began coming to the group, we eventually got together and he became my lover. All of this was done in the good mutual faith between Donald and me. He was genuinely happy for me to have these relationships, and they did not intrude upon our harmony.

However, in time, after Donald's death, it became clear to me that my relationship with Jim, especially the intimately sexual part of it, did bother Don at a level below the threshold of his awareness, or mine, for that matter. I doubt he ever realized or acknowledged the emotion. I certainly never saw any trace of it, and I am a sensitive person, able to pick up nuances of feeling. But he must have felt these things, and it led him, in the end, to lose faith in my allegiance. And that completely misplaced doubt was the weakness in his armor of light that resulted in his dying.

Long are the hours I have spent reflecting upon this matter. On the one hand, if I had been completely chaste and celibate, he would never have doubted me. He would have still been living and with me. But we would not have had the contact with Ra that gave us the Law of One material, because it was the combined energy of us three that contacted Ra, not myself as channel, or any one of us at L/L Research, or even L/L Research as an entity. This is clear from the simple dates: Jim came to L/L permanently on December 23, 1980, and we received our first contact from those of Ra on January 15, 1981, less than three weeks after Jim moved in. And Donald felt from the first session with Ra that this was his life's work, the culmination of all he had been through since the '50s, and his gift to the world. Logic fails in matters like these. One can hew completely and faithfully to the agreements one has made and still err.

If one can move beyond the mythic tragedy of Donald's death, and believe me, one can, after a decade or so, barely, one begins to see the inherent humor in that human, prideful assumption that one can control one's destiny by doing only what is seen as right. One can certainly try to be without error or sin. My pride in myself as being one who always keeps her word blinded me to the suspicions Donald had but kept completely to himself. His lack of faith in any opinion but his own, even when completely healthy of mind, made it more likely that when he became mentally ill, he would experience paranoia. It is a perfect tragedy.

Don wanted always and only my presence. He never asked for anything else, with the exception of the work we did together. He even begrudged me the time to work on his projects when he was at home. I did all the work for the books we wrote together while he was flying. When he was home, my job was to be in the same room he was in. I was delighted to do this. He could never bring himself to express it, but well I knew how devoted he was, and I felt the same. We had little choice in this; we both felt we were destined to be together, that we were truly star-crossed. Loving him was like breathing, and it did not matter how his needs impinged on mine. Indeed, my spiritual adviser said more than once that I was guilty of idolatry. I did not care what had to be lost to achieve his comfort. I knew these losses included marriage, home, and children, things I valued highly and had hoped for. But we were "home" to each other in a way I cannot describe. He rested me, and I, him. I received two compliments from him, in our whole life together. He did not want to spoil me! The lessons were to see through the issues of home, family, and reassurance to the ground of being that we shared, to the sensibility we had in common. I embraced them. He was worth whatever it cost. I look back and know I would not change anything. All our choices were made as well as we could make them.

This was the jigsaw puzzle within which we were living, in the world-drama, soap-opera consensus reality of our everyday lives. Carla and Don worked perfectly, as did Jim and Carla, and Don and Jim, who loved each other like family from the first meeting. These relationships were strong and true. Naught could have come between us except for doubt. It never occurred to me that Donald could mistake my fondness for Jim for any sort of alteration in Don's and my unmarriage version of being wed—and we were indeed truly wed, in spirit. You can imagine my wretchedness when one of his friends told me, long after the funeral, that Don had thought I had fallen out of love with him. I was flabbergasted, completely unaware of these doubts, so it never occurred to me to reassure him. How I wish I had! But I was grieving, for the man I knew was gone, and what took his place was a person in very bad need of help. And I was angry that he would not seek help or follow any medical suggestions. He was my world, and without him, I felt I did not exist. I think most of my grieving was done before his death, in those surrealistic months when he was so very ill, and nothing I did to help was of avail. It took years after he died for me to come to a new sense of myself. That I have now done so is a gift of grace from the Creator and has been greatly aided by Jim's sensitive treatment of me during the long *years of confinement with debilitating episodes of arthritis and other troubles in the decade following Don's death, and during my rehab period in 1992. For the first six years after Don died, I actively felt I should kill myself, because I had "caused" his death, inadvertently, but surely. This was my longest walk in the desert until this present moment. I was resigned to having this basic mindset for the rest of my life, and I was not aware that time had begun its healing work until I picked up something I'd written and forgot about. I read it anew, and thought, "You know, I like this person." Six years in the desert! Many were the times I was tempted to lay down my faith, but I could not, would not do that. So I survived and waited for grace. The lesson here is simply that waiting does bring all things to one. Patience cannot be overvalued in the spiritual journey.*

This world remains to me a sea of confusion. Knowing well how much I have erred, in what I have done and what I've left undone, and knowing how little I understand, I am well content to remain in the hands of destiny. One of my desires in publishing this personal material is to expose, with utter lack of modesty or fear, the humanness of the three of us. We were not "worthy" of the Ra contact, in the sense of being perfect people. We were three pilgrims who found comfort in each other, and who sought honestly and deeply to serve the light. The material is completely apart from who any of us was or is, and we are not to be confused with Ra, as having some sort of special excellence. This just is not so.

Are relative ethics OK? I still believe they are, and that keeping carefully made agreements is a real key to harmonious living and clear relationships. But it is just the best we can do. That doesn't make it perfect. Further, one cannot expect the universe to bless us with perfect peace just because we are keeping our agreements. We all are blindsided by life itself and continue only by blunder, faith, and a good humor in the face of all. There is an art to cooperating with destiny. And may I say, I am grateful to James Allen McCarty for that selfsame good humor, and for deciding with me, three years after Don's death, to take hold of our friendship and create a marriage between us. He was most ill-suited to such, as I said, and his gallant cheer and courtesy in accommodating himself to this role has been and continues to be remarkable to me. Truly, he has been a good companion through many waters.

One thing is sure: in true love, the star-crossed kind, there is incredible sweetness, but also immense pain. Don was a hard man to love. Not communicative in the usual sense, he never said what he wanted of me, but just waited for me to guess right. I did not mind and still am glad of every bit of pain I went through trying to be what he needed me to be, which was essentially without sexuality or the usual reassurance of words, yet greatly intimate. In the density we came from, we were already one, Ra said. So there was an ultimate satisfaction in being with Don, having to do much more with eternity than any particular time or space. What Jim and I had and have is the devoted love of old friends and lovers, who have an earthly pilgrimage together. Our time together is child's play after Don, as far as my being able to handle whatever happens with us. Jim will communicate until we find every bit of misunderstanding, and so we have an easy time of it, and when we do have catalyst together, it is quickly worked through. Jim's never had that ultimate romance and occasionally misses it. But what we do have is so good to us that we have found a considerable happiness with each other, and the good work we have between us.

We see ourselves as still working for and with Don, keeping L/L's doors open and our hearts as well, and living the devotional life that we have learned about from the Confederation teachings. These teachings are at one with universal wisdom as well as my Christian heritage and have to do simply with living in love. This is such a simple teaching that it escapes many people. But that focus upon Love is one's access to truth, and one's willingness to keep the heart open, which one may call faith, is the energy that brings to us all that was meant for us, both of lessons to learn and of service to offer.

And above all, we may acknowledge, for once and for all, that we are but dust, unless we are living in Love. This helps one to deal with sorrows that inevitably visit our lives. We are not supposed to be in control, or perfect, or any particular thing, but just those who continue to love, through whatever confusion there is. Sheer persistence in faith, regardless of the illusion, is the key to many blessings.

Session 18,
February 4, 1981

QUESTIONER: I was thinking last night that if I was in the place of Ra right now, the first distortion of the Law of One might cause me to mix some erroneous data with the true information that I was transmitting to this group. Do you do this?

RA: I am Ra. We do not intentionally do this. However, there will be confusion. The errors which have occurred have occurred due to the occasional variation in the vibrational complex of this instrument due to its ingestion of a chemical substance. It is not our intent in this particular project to create erroneous information, but to express in the confining ambiance of your language system the feeling of the infinite mystery of the one creation in its infinite and intelligent unity.

QUESTIONER: Can you tell me what the chemical substance is that, when ingested, causes poor contact?

RA: I am Ra. This is not a clear query. Could you please restate.

QUESTIONER: You just stated that you had some problems with the instrument because of the ingestion of some chemical substance by the instrument. Can you tell me what the chemical substance was?

RA: I am Ra. The substance of which we speak is called vibration sound complex LSD. It does not give poor contact if it is used in conjunction with the contact. The difficulty of this particular substance is that there is, shall we say, a very dramatic drop-off of the effect of this substance. In each case this instrument began the session with the distortion towards extreme vital energy which this substance produces. However, this entity was, during the session, at the point where this substance no longer was in sufficient strength to amplify the entity's abilities to express vital energy. Thus, first the phenomenon of, shall we say, a spotty contact and then, as the instrument relies again upon its own vibrational complexes of vital energy, the vital energy in this case being very low, it became necessary to abruptly cut off communication in order to preserve and nurture the instrument. This particular chemical substance is both helpful and unhelpful in these contacts for the causes given.

QUESTIONER: Are there any foods that are helpful or harmful that the instrument might eat?

RA: I am Ra. This instrument has body complex distortion towards ill health in the distortion direction corrected best by ingestion of the foodstuffs of your grains and your vegetables, as you call them. However, this is extremely unimportant when regarded as an aid with equality to other aids such as attitude, which this instrument has in abundance. It, however, aids the vital energies of this instrument, with less distortion towards ill health, to ingest foodstuffs in the above manner, with the occasional ingestion of what you call your meats, due to the instrument's need to lessen the distortion towards low vital energy.

QUESTIONER: The entity Aleister Crowley wrote, "Do what thou wilt is the whole of the law." He was obviously of some understanding of the Law of One. Where is this entity now?

RA: I am Ra. This entity is within your inner planes. This entity is in an healing process.

QUESTIONER: Did this entity, then, even though he intellectually understood the Law of One, misuse it and have to go through this healing process?

RA: I am Ra. This entity became, may we use the vibration sound complex, overstimulated with the true nature of things. This overstimulation resulted in behavior that was beyond the conscious control of the entity. The entity thus, in many attempts to go through the process of balancing, as we have described the various centers beginning with the red ray and moving upwards, became somewhat overly impressed or caught up in this process and became alienated from other-selves. This entity was positive. However, its journey was difficult due to the inability to use, synthesize, and harmonize the understandings of the desires of self so that it might have shared, in full compassion, with other-selves. This entity thus became very unhealthy, as you may call it, in a spiritual complex manner, and it is necessary for those with this type of distortion towards inner pain to be nurtured in the inner planes until such an entity is capable of viewing the experiences again with the lack of distortion towards pain.

QUESTIONER: I just have two little questions here at the end. The instrument wanted to ask if there were any other substances, foods, etc., that she should not eat or drink, or things that she should not do because she does not wish to have poor contact for any reason.

RA: I am Ra. There is no activity which this instrument engages in which affects abilities negatively. There is one activity which affects its abilities positively. This is the sexual activity, as you would call it. There are substances ingested which do not aid the individual in the service it has chosen, this being that which you would call the marijuana. This is due to the distortion towards chemical lapses within the mind complex, causing lack of synaptic continuity. This is a chemical reaction of short duration. This instrument, however, has not used this particular substance at any time while performing this service. We believe we have covered the use of such chemical agents as LSD, this being positive to a certain extent due to the energizing or speeding up of the vital forces. However, it is not recommended for this instrument due to the toll it takes upon the vital energies once the substance wears off. This being true of any speeding-up chemical.

Fragment 10

As we were preparing to welcome Dr. Puharich into our circle of working with Ra, we were reminded once again of the prerequisite of the tuning in the personal life that was necessary for all of those involved in the contact.

In the event, Andrija never visited us here in Kentucky. But it is worth noting that Ra frequently did respond to our questions by invoking the law of confusion. Those of Ra felt that the primary importance in personal ethics of allowing people to do their own learning, make their own mistakes, cannot be overemphasized.

Session 21,
February 10, 1981

QUESTIONER: Andrija Puharich will be visiting later this month. Can he read the unpublished healing material?

RA: I am Ra. The entity of whom you speak has a knowledge of this material in its conscious memory in somewhat altered form. Therefore, it is harmless to allow this entity to become acquainted with this material. However, we request the mind/body/spirit complex, Henry, be sufficiently prepared by means of meditation, contemplation, or prayer before entering these workings. At present, as we have said before, this mind/body/spirit complex is not of proper vibrational distortion.

QUESTIONER: I had already determined to exclude him from these workings. I had only determined to let him read the material. The only other thing that I have noticed within the material as it exists now is that there is a certain statement that will allow him to understand who I believe Spectra really was. It seems to be my duty to remove this from his knowledge to preserve the same free will that you attempted to preserve by not naming the origin of the Spectra contact in Israel. Am I correct?

RA: I am Ra. This is a matter for your discretion.

QUESTIONER: That's what I thought you'd say.

Fragment 11
Most of the personal information from Session 22 is self-explanatory. The prayer that Ra speaks of in relation to Carla is the Prayer of St. Francis, which Carla has used as her own personal tuning mechanism

since she began channeling in 1974. It further refines the tuning done by the support group and is always prayed mentally before any session, whether telepathic or trance.

The limitations of which Ra speaks in the second answer refer to Carla's rheumatoid arthritis, which was apparently chosen before the incarnation to provide an inner focus for her meditative work rather than to allow the ease of outer expression that might have dissipated the inner orientation. Thus, not all disabilities are meant to yield to even the best efforts of healers, and when such a disability does not respond to any kind of healing effort, one may begin to consider what opportunities for learning and service are opened up by the disability. Ra even mentioned in the last sentence that her acceptance of her disabilities and limitations would ease the amount of pain that she suffered because of them.

It was distinctly odd to be going about and walking into aromas that had no overt origin. It seemed to me throughout this time that I was being more and more sensitized, and less and less vibrating with my humanhood. I feel sure that the constant weight loss added to this Alice in Wonderland feeling. To the present day, I continue to have a very sensitized physical vehicle. However, my formerly tiny body has grown from size preteen 5/8 to its present position athwart 14/16, a weight gain of double the lightest weight reached during the contact. Just for a feel for where "normal" is for me, I used to weigh between 115 and 120, year after year. I looked quite normal at that weight. It's been interesting to feel the different weights I have been, to live with a more or less bulky vehicle. One feels stronger, the heavier one is. I was surprised at this, figuring that lighter weights would make one feel more toned and vital. It makes it easier to understand why we in America so often allow ourselves to eat to the point of obesity. It feels good! One doubts that it is a life-lengthening thing, however!

The pre-incarnative choice that I made to have a body that would limit what I could do is one I have taken a long time to appreciate. It is frustrating at first not to be able to do the work one's trained to do. I loved being a librarian; I enjoyed researching for Don. When I could no longer work in these ways, I was profoundly puzzled and not a little upset. But then, quiet years taught me so much. I learned the open heart although my body was declining; I found hope and faith although the physical picture grew steadily worse. After Donald died, I came close to dying too, and in 1992, when at last I was able to turn the boat around, I felt the grip of death loosen and fall away.

My present experience is of living in a barely working physical vehicle. Taking no less than seven medications, I walk the razor's edge between doing too much and not doing enough. The one thing that has never changed throughout this experience is my dedication to helping the Wanderers of this planet. All the various skills that I have had to give up have their place in my work with people who are having trouble with their spiritual path, and so I feel fully useful at last. And yet I know that we are all most useful, not by what we do or say, but in the quality of our being.

Session 22,
February 10, 1981

QUESTIONER: The instrument would like to ask a couple of questions of you. The instrument would like to know why she smells the incense at various times during the day at various places.

RA: I am Ra. This instrument has spent a lifetime in dedication to service. This has brought this instrument to this nexus in space/time with the conscious and unconscious distortion towards service, with the further conscious distortion towards service by communication. Each time, as you would put it, that we perform this working, our social memory complex vibrational distortion meshes more firmly with this instrument's unconscious distortions towards service. Thus we are becoming a part of this instrument's vibratory complex, and it, a part of ours. This occurs upon the unconscious level, the level whereby the mind has gone down through to the roots of consciousness which you may call cosmic. This instrument is not consciously aware of this slow changing of the meshing vibratory complex. However, as the dedication on both levels continues, and the workings continue, there are signals sent from the unconscious in a symbolic manner. Because this instrument is extremely keen in its sense of smell, this association takes place unconsciously, and the thought-form of this odor is witnessed by the entity.

QUESTIONER: Secondly, she would like to know why she feels more healthy now that she has begun these sessions and feels more healthy as time goes on.

RA: I am Ra. This is a function of the free will of the entity. This entity has, for many of your years, prayed a certain set of sound vibration complexes before opening to communication. Before the trance state was achieved, this prayer remained within the conscious portion of the mind complex and, though helpful, was not as effective as the consequence of this prayer, as you would call this vibrational sound complex, which then goes directly into the unconscious level, thus more critically affecting the communication from the spiritual complex. Also, this entity has begun, due to this working, to accept certain limitations which it placed upon itself in order to set the stage for services such as it now performs. This also is an aid to realigning the distortions of the physical complex with regard to pain.

Fragment 12
Dr. Puharich never did visit us during the Ra contact, so all of our questions about how he should prepare for joining the contact were only for our information. His strong desire to solve riddles and puzzles and his desire to prove spiritual truth would have made it difficult for him to become a part of our circle, since it was supported by the opposite mental attitude, faith.

Once one starts watching for synchronicities, one can find many a book, movie, or any other object or event bringing repeated messages and reminders of our path. So often, Jim and I will be discussing an issue only to find that for the next day or two, we receive confirmations meaningful only to us.

And I do think that many wanderers here are making today's movies and songs. One has only to listen to the wonderful words to current songs, sung by people as diverse as Arlo Guthrie and Donovan, Black Oak Arkansas and Earth, Wind and Fire, the Rolling Stones . . . the list is as long as my legs! We have wonderful company, we who wander here on earth.

Session 23,
February 11, 1981

QUESTIONER: I can't answer this question but I will ask it anyway, since we are in the area that I think that this occurred in. I feel this is somewhat of a duty to ask this question because Henry Puharich will be visiting us here later this month. Was this entity involved in any of these times of which you have just spoken?

RA: I am Ra. You are quite correct in your assumption that we can speak in no way concerning the entity Henry. If you will consider this entity's distortions with regard to what you call "proof," you will understand/grasp our predicament.

QUESTIONER: I had assumed before I asked the question that that would be the answer. I only asked it for his benefit because he wished for me to. This may be a dumb question. There is a movie called *Battle Beyond the Stars*. I don't know if you are familiar with it or not. I guess you are. It just seemed to have what you are telling us included in the script. Is this correct?

RA: I am Ra. This particular creation of your entities had some distortions of the Law of One and its scenario upon your physical plane. This is correct.

Fragment 13

The following information refers to two of the most widely rumored events in ufology in this country. The first refers to the supposed face-to-face meeting between extraterrestrials and then president Dwight D. Eisenhower and some senior military staff at Edwards Air Force Base in California in February 1954. The second incident refers to the supposed crash of a UFO outside Roswell, New Mexico, in which the ufonauts onboard supposedly died. It is further rumored that their bodies were stored in Hangar #18 at Wright-Patterson Air Force Base in Ohio. Once again we encountered the temptation to pursue information that seemed on the surface to be extremely interesting, but which in truth would yield little or no information that might aid in the evolution of mind, body, or spirit. And we would have lost the Ra contact because Ra's "narrow-band contact" was focused only on aiding our evolution and not on revealing the transient intricacies of how groups play games in this illusion.

In 1962, when I joined with Donald to help make up the initial meditation group that grew into L/L Research, there were several rumors being bruited about. Supposedly, the government knew all about UFOs, had had contact. There were alleged conspiracies that various sources warned the public about. To this day, there has continued a steady stream of such prophecies and doomsday warnings of all kinds. Only the dates of Armageddon have changed, usually predicting doom within the next two or three years.

It is not that I do not think UFOs are communicating with our government. They might be. Certainly they are here; the landing-trace cases alone prove that something that makes dents in the ground is visiting us, and the many witnesses and abductees create a comprehensive picture of human-alien contact that is undeniable. It is that I feel that the real treasure the UFO entities have brought us are those of the spirit, not those of this world. Whatever the physical reality of UFOs and governmental doings, they remain part of the transient world picture: part of this heavy illusion. But the messages have a metaphysical content that 10,000 years would not make out of date or less meaningful. So I tend to respond to people's questions about such hijinks as these with a redirection, back from phenomena to metaphysical truth.

Session 24,
February 15, 1981

QUESTIONER: One thing that has been bothering me that I was just reading about is not too important, but I would really be interested in knowing if Dwight Eisenhower met with either the Confederation or the Orion group in the 1950s?

RA: I am Ra. The one of which you speak met with thought-forms which are indistinguishable from third density. This was a test. We, the Confederation, wished to see what would occur if this extremely positively oriented and simple congenial person with no significant distortion towards power happened across peaceful information and the possibilities which might append therefrom. We discovered that this entity did not feel that those under his care could deal with the concepts of other beings and other philosophies. Thus, an agreement reached then allowed him to go his way—ourselves to do likewise—and a very quiet campaign, as we have heard you call it, be continued alerting your peoples to our presence gradually. Events have overtaken this plan. Is there any short query before we close?

QUESTIONER: Another question with that is, was there a crashed spaceship with small bodies now stored in our military installations?

RA: I am Ra. We do not wish to infringe upon your future. Gave we you this information, we might be giving you more than you could appropriately deal with in the space/time nexus of your present somewhat muddled configuration of military and intelligence thought. Therefore, we shall withhold this information.

Fragment 14
The following information gave us some insight into how one's choices can be used in either the positive or the negative sense, even when there is the seeming interference of negative entities in the manner of what many light workers call psychic attack, and what we came to call psychic greetings. We chose the term "greeting" to emphasize that there does not have to be a negative experience on the part of the one

who is greeted, and that the experience that the one who is greeted actually has is in direct proportion to how that entity looks at the situation. If one wishes to see such a greeting as a difficult attack, then that becomes the experience. One can, however, also choose to see the Creator in all entities and events and can praise and seek the light within any situation, and then that will tend to become the experience.

When this latter choice is made, the psychic greeting becomes a great blessing in that it presents to the one who is greeted an intensive opportunity to see the One Creator where it may be more difficult to see, and which, when accomplished, develops a great deal more spiritual strength than may normally be developed without the negative entity's aid in pointing out the weaker areas of our magical personalities. Psychic greetings can only be offered by negative entities enhancing our own free will choices that are distorted toward service-to-self thought and behavior. Our poor choices, usually reflecting a lack of love toward another or the self, get magnified by the negative entity and bleed away our efforts to seek the light and serve others until we are able to balance the situation with love, acceptance, compassion, tolerance, and the light touch. This is why Jesus said to "resist not evil." To resist and fight is to see someone or something as other than the self, as other than the One Creator. That is the negative path. The positive path sees and loves all as the self and as the One.

The work that was perforce mine during this time of psychic greeting was, as Jim pointed out, very helpful in focusing my will and attention. I remember feeling tremendously uplifted and held in safe hands through all of the episodes. The key was the surrender to seeing one's own dark side. I think Dion Fortune's description of how to deal with a vampiric entity, in that case a wolf, still to be the most direct example of the understanding needed to move through such times. This wise soul had a wolf appearing at her bed, during training in white Western ritual magic. The solution was to draw the wolf directly into the breast, loving it and accepting it as self. Against fearless love, the powers of negation and death are helpless and melt away.

I think those of Ra were very careful of our group, compared to some sources, who did not show much concern that they were wearing the instrument out. Advice such as was given for me could well apply to anyone who must husband one's energy.

Session 25,
February 16, 1981

QUESTIONER: What cause or complex of causes has led to the instrument's chest cold, as it is called?

RA: I am Ra. This distortion towards illness was caused by the free will of the instrument in accepting a chemical substance which you call LSD. This was carefully planned by those entities which do not desire this instrument to remain viable. The substance has within it the facility of removing large stores of vital energy from the ingestor. The first hope of the Orion entity which arranged this opportunity was that this instrument would become less polarized towards what you call the positive. Due to conscious efforts upon the part of this instrument, using the substance as a programmer for service to others and for thankfulness, this instrument was spared this distortion and there was no result satisfactory to the Orion group.

The second hope lay in the possible misuse of the most-powerful means of transmission of energy between your peoples in the area of body complex distortions. We have not previously spoken of the various types of energy blockages and transfers, positive and negative, that may take place due to participation in your sexual-reproductive complex of actions. This entity, however, is a very strong entity with very little distortion from universal green-ray love energy. Thus this particular plan was not effected either, as the entity continued to give of itself in this context in an open or green-ray manner rather than attempting to deceive or to manipulate other-self.

The only remaining distortion available, since this entity would not detune and would not cease sharing love universally under this chemical substance, was simply to drain this entity of as much energy as possible. This entity has a strong distortion towards busyness which it has been attempting to overcome for some time, realizing it not to be the appropriate attitude for this work. In this particular area the ingestion of this substance did indeed, shall we say, cause distortions away from viability due to the busyness and the lack of desire to rest; this instrument staying alert for much longer than appropriate. Thus much vital energy was lost, making this instrument unusually susceptible to infections such as it now experiences.

QUESTIONER: The second question that the instrument requested is: How may I best revitalize myself not only now but in the future?

RA: I am Ra. This instrument is aware of the basic needs of its constitution, those being meditation, acceptance of limitations, experiences of joy through association with others, and with the beauty as of the singing, and the exercising with great contact, whenever possible, with the life forces of second density, especially those of trees; this entity also needing to be aware of the moderate but steady intake of foodstuffs, exercise being suggested at a fairly early portion of the day and at a later portion of the day before the resting.

QUESTIONER: The third question that she requested was: How may Don and Jim help to revitalize me?

RA: I am Ra. This is not an appropriate question for full answer. We can say only that these entities are most conscientious. We may add that due to this instrument's distortion towards imbalance in the space/time nexus, it would be well were this entity accompanied during exercise.

Fragment 15

The following information refers again to Carla's two experiences with LSD. We were very thankful that there were only two experiences with which she and we had to deal, for, as you can see, the debilitating effects apparently mount rapidly with each ingestion. The sessions in Book II of *The Law of One* were necessarily shortened in order to conserve the vital energy of the instrument, which had been drained by the LSD.

I can only add the fact that this period of weakness did occur, and so Ra's suggestion not to mix any drugs with channeling seems to me a sound piece of advice that I have followed ever since.

Session 26,
February 17, 1981

QUESTIONER: The instrument asks how long will the debilitating effects that I am experiencing due to the LSD last, and is there anything that we can do to make the instrument more comfortable?

RA: I am Ra. Firstly, the period of weakness of bodily complex is approximately three of your lunar cycles: the first ingestion causing approximately one of your lunar cycles; the second having a cumulative or doubling effect.

Fragment 16

Just before I joined Don and Carla, at the end of 1980, I traveled to the Portland, Oregon, area to work with Paul Shockley and the Aquarian Church of Universal Service. It was a happy experience in itself, and it also provided the catalyst that eventually saw me return to Kentucky and join L/L Research. After two months in Oregon I decided to take a weekend alone to think about an opportunity to earn a great deal of money that had been presented to me by one of the members of the Aquarian Church. Thirty seconds into my first meditation of the weekend, the very clear message to return to Don and Carla flashed across my inner sky. So I said goodbye to my new friends and returned to Louisville. Three weeks later the Ra contact began, and when Paul Shockley was informed of the nature of the contact, he asked that two questions be asked for him of the social memory complex Ra.

The answer to the second query is especially interesting to us because it seems to suggest the means by which some of the pyramids of Egypt were constructed.

In 1986, we were invited to Shockley's "Friendship" conference, and I finally met this channel for a source called "Cosmic Awareness." He was a very sincere and valiant channel, pure in his desire to serve. I feel it unfortunate that the questions put to this channel, over a period of time, pretty much changed and worsened the quality of information received. As always when this occurs, the culprit was a fascination with transient material. I think that it was the questions put to this excellent channel that lessened the metaphysical level of this channeling.

Session 27,
February 21, 1981

QUESTIONER: Jim has felt the obligation to ask two questions that were asked of him by Paul Shockley, and I will ask those two first, in case you are able to answer them before we get started. The first question: Paul Shockley is presently channeling the same source which Edgar Cayce channeled, and he has received information that he took part in the design and construction of the Egyptian pyramids. Can you tell us what his role was in that effort?

RA: I am Ra. This was in your space/time continuum two periods and two lifetimes. The first of a physical nature working with Confederation entities in what you know as Atlantis, this approximately 13,000 of your years ago. This memory, shall we say, being integrated into the unconscious of the mind/body/spirit complex of this entity due to its extreme desire to remember the service of healing and polarization possible by the mechanisms of the crystal and the charged healer.

The second experience being approximately 1,000 of your years later, during which experience this entity prepared, in some part, the consciousness of the people of what you now call Egypt, that they were able to offer the calling that enabled those of our social memory complex to walk among your peoples. During this life experience, this entity was of a priest and teaching nature and succeeded in remembering in semidistorted form the learn/teachings of the Atlantean pyramidal experiences. Thus, this entity became a builder of the archetypal thought of the Law of One with distortions towards healing, which aided our people in bringing this through into a physical manifestation.

QUESTIONER: The second question is: Paul has also received information that there were other beings aiding in the construction of the pyramids, but that they were not fully materialized in the third density. They were materialized from their waist up to their heads but were not materialized from their waist down to their feet. Did such entities exist and aid in the construction of the pyramids, and who were they?

RA: I am Ra. Consider, if you will, the intelligent infinity present in the absorption of livingness and beingness as it becomes codified into intelligent energy, due to the thought impressions of those assisting the living stone into a new shape of beingness. The release and use of intelligent infinity for a brief period begins to absorb all the consecutive or interlocking dimensions, thus offering brief glimpses of those projecting to the material their thought. These beings thus beginning to materialize but not remaining visible. These beings were the thought-form or third-density visible manifestation of our social memory complex as we offered contact from our intelligent infinity to the intelligent infinity of the stone.

Fragment 17

Ra had advised Carla never to do any kind of physical healing, because she was always very low on physical energy, and such healing would tend to drain her already low reserve in that area.

Since I was a child, I have had some sort of odd ability to sit with someone and, with our hands in contact, be able to clear some of the surface clutter away from the other person's mind or being. I have never investigated what

I am doing or how to do it better, trusting rather in my instinct for the right time to offer this. Perhaps I should, but it has always struck me as a very marginal gift, not one near my central path. I think that if I have any healing ability, it is in my listening. When someone comes to me for private counsel, I think of the time as a "listening session" and see myself as a spiritual listener. There is much healing in a person's talking something through with another in a supportive atmosphere. The listener simply enables the person to listen better to herself. And I have very deep instincts toward doing this. So this is where I have focused my own efforts to become a better healer. Listening is truly an art, and I think it begins with the way we listen to ourselves. There is a tremendous strength in knowing one's full self, the dark side as well as the one that sees the light of everyday behavior.

Once one has finally become able to bear one's own full nature and has gone through the painful process of surrendering the pride that would deny that wretchedness within, one becomes better able to love and forgive oneself. Often I think we feel our failure comes in being unkind to another. But when this occurs, you can be sure the first and proximate cause of this outer ruthlessness lies within, in the self's refusal to reckon with the full-circle self.

Session 29,
February 23, 1981

QUESTIONER: The instrument had a question, if we have time for a short question. I will read it. The instrument does not desire to do physical-healing work. She already does spiritual balancing by hands. Can she read the private healing material without doing physical healing? I am assuming that she means can she read it without creating problems in her life pattern. She does not wish to incur lessening of positive polarity. Can she read the material under these conditions?

RA: I am Ra. We shall speak shortly due to the fact that we are attempting to conserve this instrument's vital energies during the three-month period of which we have spoken.

This entity has an experiential history of healing on levels other than the so-called physical. Thus it is acceptable that this material be read. However, the exercise of fire shall never be practiced by this instrument, as it is used in the stronger form for physical healing.

Fragment 18
A fellow associated with Cosmic Awareness Communications in

Washington State was developing and distributing a machine that was supposed to augment the general health and well-being of a person, and we asked Ra whether it might aid Carla. The response suggested that Carla's magnetic field was somewhat unusual and very likely formed in such an unusual way as to permit contact with those of Ra specifically. This unusual magnetic field has been a source of frequent inconveniences with any electromagnetic equipment that Carla has used on a regular basis. She breaks it—just by touching it periodically. She can't wear any but quartz crystal watches, and we have many, many semifunctional tape recorders lying about different areas of our house.

It makes for a good story, but it can be frustrating to have electronically damaging energy—I am not amused when I break things. The last thing I want to do is destroy the very machines that allow me to communicate. And my tendency to feel various odd energies has at times been an unwelcome gift. I remember a couple of times when my being able to perceive some occult frequency or another put me in the way of very forceful people who decided that I was to work with them. Of course, I have withstood any requests for help that I felt uncomfortable accepting, but I really don't enjoy the process of convincing someone that I won't come out and play!

In all of the things, and there are a million or two, that we've tried to better my physical condition, we have not found anything of that nature that avails. However, the gifts of spirit and faith are far more efficacious. So I have become relatively uninterested in new modalities and gadgets— and rest in prayer and peace, knowing the perfect self within.

Session 30,
February 24, 1981

QUESTIONER: The instrument would like to know if you could tell her whether or not this item which is called Sam Millar's polarizer would help her physical well-being. Could you do that?

RA: I am Ra. As we scan the instrument, we find anomalies of the magnetic field which are distorted towards our abilities to find narrow-band channel into this instrument's mind/body/spirit complex. The polarizer of which you speak, as it is, would not be helpful. A careful reading of this instrument's aura by those gifted in this area, and subsequent alterations of the magnetizing forces of this polarizer, would assist the entity, Sam, in creating such a polarizer that would be of some aid to the instrument. However, we would suggest that no electrical or magnetic equipment not necessary for the recording of our words be brought into these sessions, for we wish no distortions that are not necessary.

Fragment 19
Many people have written to us over the years, telling us of what they call psychic attacks and asking how to protect themselves from them. It seems that one needn't perform any elaborate rituals or call upon any big-league light bearers for assistance. Ra describes the manner in which anyone can provide all the protection that will ever be necessary in any situation. And it is very, very simple.

I will be 54 next birthday, and as I get older, I become more and more convinced that our path always lies in offering praise and thanksgiving for whatever is coming our way, no matter what we may humanly think about it. This is easy to do in good times, but it is a matter of some persistence of discipline to train the mind not to shrink away from trouble we perceive coming at us. However, I encourage in everyone that patient tenacity that refuses to doubt the Creator, no matter what. Once we have very clear the fact that we are safely in the Creator's hands and heart, this becomes easier. But the work is never fully done, for we fail again and again to witness to the light, and this causes confusion in our patterns of destiny.

Session 32,
February 27, 1981

QUESTIONER: I have a question that I will throw in at this point from Jim. I will read it. The instrument's physical vehicle is now in the process of recovery from the ingestion of a chemical. She was ignorant of the opening that she was creating. How may the three of us present be more aware of how such openings may be created in our actions and our thoughts? Is it possible that we can make such openings innocently as we question in different areas during these sessions? And what can we do to protect ourselves from negative influences in general? Are there any rituals or meditations that we can do to protect ourselves?

RA: I am Ra. Although we are in sympathy with the great desire to be of service exemplified by the question, our answer is limited by the distortion of the Way of Confusion. We shall say some general things which may be of service in this area.

Firstly, when this instrument distorted its bodily complex towards low vital energy due to this occurrence, it was a recognizable substance which caused this. This was not a, shall we say, natural substance nor was the mind/body/spirit complex enough aware of its distortion towards physical weakness. The natural ways of, shall we say, everyday existence, in which the entity without the distortions caused by ingestion of strongly effective chemicals, may be seen to be of an always appropriate nature. There are no mistakes, including the action of this instrument.

Secondly, the means of protection against any negative or debilitating influence for those upon the positive path was demonstrated by this instrument to a very great degree. Consider, if you will, the potentials that this particular occurrence had for negative influences to enter the instrument. This instrument thought upon the Creator in its solitude and in actions with other-self, continually praised and gave thanksgiving to the Creator for the experiences it was having. This in turn allowed this particular self such energies as became a catalyst for an opening and strengthening of the other-self's ability to function in a more positively polarized state. Thus we see protection being very simple. Give thanksgiving for each moment. See the self and the other-self as Creator. Open the heart. Always know the light and praise it. This is all the protection necessary.

Fragment 20

Because Carla's physical energy level was always very low and constantly being drained by the arthritic condition and the persistent presence of some degree of pain, it became necessary for her to engage in daily exercise in order to maintain the function of each portion of her body. We found that the more distorted or low on energy she was, the greater was the need for this exercise. When her body was functioning most nearly normally, the exercise could be reduced in length until it also was normal. For Carla that was about one hour of rapid walking per day.

When Don queried about an experience that he had in 1964, the specificity of the answer was limited by Ra's desire to maintain Don's free will. Most events in our lives are a mystery in some degree or another. One way of looking at the process of evolution is to see it as the process of solving the mysteries all about us. All events are illusions or mysteries because each represents the One Creator in one disguise or another, offering us a greater or lesser opportunity to find love, joy, balance, and perfection in each moment. There is a spiritual strength that comes with unraveling such mysteries for one's self. It is not always a service for those with better-trained eyes to tell another what he does not yet see for himself, but which he has the capacity to learn to see. Thus Ra often invoked the Law of Free Will, also known as the Law of Confusion.

When I was a child, I danced and swam and rode horses. I loved exercise, especially when it was rhythmic. The exercise that was my lot to do during this time was, though very hard because I felt so tired, an energizing experience. Both Don and Jim helped me remember to get these periods in, and Jim made them easier still by joining me. It is always easier to do such things with a buddy! Don was not able to join me in these walks, as he had a painful condition of the feet brought on by working in tropical climes, and every step hurt. However, I witnessed, from time to time, a level of animal strength in Don that was miraculous. For instance, in 1977 Don and I went to join in a Mind Link held by Andrija Puharich. Gathered were a mixed bag of established psychics, all women, and other middle-aged supporters, and about an equal number of college-age kids who had identified themselves to Puharich as Wanderers. The kids loved soccer and played it when we weren't in session. Don joined in their first game. He did really well, impressing not only me but all the kids. They finally had to stop the game, red faced and panting. Donald was not even breathing heavily. Needless to say, the kids warmed up to Don quickly! But they never could get him to play again.

Session 34,
March 4, 1981

QUESTIONER: The instrument would like to know if two short exercise periods per day would be better for her than one long one.

RA: I am Ra. This is incorrect. The proper configuration of the physical complex exercising during the three-month period, wherein the instrument is vulnerable to physical complex distortion intensification, needs the strengthening of the physical complex. This may appropriately be seen to be one major period of the exercising, followed late in your diurnal cycle before the evening meditation by an exercise period approximately one-half the length of the first. This will be seen to be wearing upon the instrument. However, it will have the effect of strengthening the physical complex and lessening the vulnerability which might be taken advantage of.

QUESTIONER: Is it possible for you to tell me what I experienced, around 1964 I believe it was, when in meditation I became aware of what I considered a different density and different planet and seemed to experience moving onto that planet? Is it possible for you to tell me what experience that was?

RA: I am Ra. We see some harm in full disclosure due to infringement. We content ourselves with suggesting that this entity, which is not readily able to subject itself to the process of hypnotic regression instigated by others, nevertheless has had its opportunities for understanding of its beingness.

Fragment 21

Having only a faint but persistent idea that we had come to this planet in order to be of service to others was apparently a sufficient degree of the "penetrating of the forgetting process" that Don mentioned in Session 36, for we had little more than that with which to begin the Ra contact.

Any third-density entity apparently has a Higher Self or Oversoul that is at the mid-sixth-density level of being. In addition, the Wanderer who is a member of a social memory complex also has another complex of consciousness upon which to call for assistance, for each social memory complex also seems to have the equivalent of its own Oversoul, or what Ra calls a "mind/body/spirit complex totality."

The forgetting process, or the veil, is a term used often by our sources. The basic thought is that when we take on flesh and become a manifested entity on the earth plane, that flesh shuts our metaphysical senses. All that we knew before birth is hidden in the deeper mind, and we set out on our earthly pilgrimage with only our naked selves and our heartfelt desires. It is no wonder then that Wanderers have some difficulty waking up within the illusion we call consensus reality. There is always the fear, as one enters incarnation, that one will not awaken at all but be lost for the whole life experience. You who read this sentence are probably right in the midst of this awakening process, beginning more and more to identify with a new and larger concept of the self as an eternal and metaphysical being.

As we all awaken and develop our truer selves, we can help each other, and I encourage each Wanderer to find ways to support fellow pilgrims of the light. People will come your way. They may not seem to be very "aware," or they may seem quite aware but very confused or frightened. If the Creator put them in your way, then you are well equipped to aid them. Simply love and accept them.

This is much harder to do than to say. It involves first coming to love and accept yourself, forgiving yourself for the myriad imperfections and folly you find when gazing within. But all work is upon the self, speaking metaphysically. If you have trouble loving someone, look within for the place within self where you have rejected part of yourself, some slice of the dark side you'd rather not see or experience. As you work with this loving, accepting, and forgiving of the dark side of self, you are working on service to all the other selves coming your way. I think the key to this acceptance of self is to see that to be in flesh is to be very imperfect and confused. There is no way to be without error when in the context of the world. Yet, within us there is that self without the veil, with perfect memory of who we are and what we came to do. Once one is able to face one's wretched side, one becomes much more able to be transparent to that infinite love that comes not from us but through us, to bless all.

In this practice of loving, we have a wonderful source of strength and courage: the Higher Self. I call this self the Holy Spirit, because I am of the distortion called mystical Christianity. Other people refer to this Higher Self as inner guides, angelic beings, the higher nature, or simply Guidance. Whatever the term, this energy is quite dependable, always there, supporting and sustaining. One can practice becoming more aware of this energy, consciously opening to it within meditation, and calling upon it in times of challenge. I encourage each to see the self as an awakening being, with much support from the unseen forces. Lean into these sources of strength in silence and prayer. They will truly aid you.

Session 36,
March 10, 1981

QUESTIONER: I was wondering if qualification for contact with Ra might include penetrating this forgetting process. Is this correct?

RA: I am Ra. This is quite correct.

QUESTIONER: Otherwise the Law of Confusion would prohibit this? Is this correct?

RA: This is correct.

QUESTIONER: I was also wondering if three was the minimum number necessary for this type of working. Is this correct?

RA: I am Ra. For protection of this instrument, this is necessary as the minimum grouping and also as the most efficient number due to the exceptional harmony in this group. In other groups the number could be larger, but we have observed in this contact that the most efficient support is given by the individual mind/body/spirits present at this time.

QUESTIONER: I'm a little fuzzy on a point with respect to the Higher Self. We each, I am assuming, have an individual Higher Self at sixth-density positive level. Is this correct? Each of us in the room here; that is, the three of us?

RA: I am Ra. This shall be the last full question of this working. We shall attempt to aim for the intention of your query as we understand it. Please request any additional information.

Firstly, it is correct that each in this dwelling place has one Oversoul, as you may call it. However, due to the repeated harmonious interactions of this triad of entities, there may be seen to be a further harmonious interaction besides the three entities' Higher Selves; that is, each social memory complex has an Oversoul of a type which is difficult to describe to you in words. In this group there are two such social memory complex totalities blending their efforts with your Higher Selves at this time.

Fragment 22

In March 1981, we sent off the first ten sessions of the Ra contact to the Scott Meredith Literary Agency in New York City. We wanted to get the information out to as many people as we could, and we thought that a large literary agency could help us find a publisher. After considering the manuscript for about two weeks, Mr. Meredith was kind enough to write us a four-page, single-spaced letter thanking us for sending him the material and telling us why it had no chance in the marketplace. The heart of the letter may be summarized by the following quote:

"No entity that wreaks such havoc with the English language is going to ingratiate himself with the general reading public. This has all the denseness of *The New England Journal of Medicine*, or the *Journal of English and German Philology*, or a PhD dissertation on epistemology . . . and for another thing, the dialogue form gets pretty tedious after a while. It was all the rage in Athens for a while, I know, and its popularity continued all the way through the Neoclassic Renaissance, but it died out shortly afterwards, and I don't think that it's about to be revived."

Ra's final comment on the topic of how to make the information available brought a somewhat humorous end to our earnestness. A few days earlier we had been sitting around the kitchen table, wondering aloud what cosmic humor might be like, and Ra took this opportunity to give us an illustration. We would give the same basic advice to any group trying to disseminate information that it has collected so that it might be of service to others. Relax, and let the Law of Attraction work. Even if only one person is aided by the work, that is enough. At the very least, the benefit that the material provides to the group alone will become like unto a light that each in the group will radiate to all others met in the daily round of activities.

And since we had discovered for ourselves the necessity of pursuing nontransient information, Ra clearly states that that was a requirement for maintaining the contact, in contrast to Don's estimate of the kind of information that usually attracts the attention of the marketplace.

It was always a hope of Don's that we would be able to communicate to a large number of people. He felt a real urgency at getting the word out, and as the contact with Ra persisted, his concern deepened. It was like a breath of fresh air to find Ra counseling us to be content with our "reasonable effort." As we write these comments, the first book of The Law of One series has sold about 30,000 copies. Our mail this week included queries from Poland, Romania, Malaysia, and Japan, as well as the USA and Canada. I am sure that a little part of Don is sitting on my shoulder like the angel he is, content at last with his life's work and seeing it taken up by those who find it useful.

The concept of sacrifice as part of the beginning of contact is not new at all. The channel for Oahspe was told in a vision that he must live austerely for ten years before he could be of help, and he and a friend did just that, living monastically, waiting for the time of opportunity. When his decade of sacrifice was through, he was told to get a typewriter, new at the time. He did so. Over the next few years, he channeled the huge book, being put at the typewriter while he was asleep at night. He would awaken each morning to find his work lying by the machine. And Edgar Cayce had similar experiences with being told he needed to sacrifice in order to serve. In our case, Jim sacrificed his love of isolation and retreat from humankind; Don sacrificed his solitude with me, that happy and safe harbor we had made together. He let Jim into the very fabric of our lives, with never the first word of complaint. He also sacrificed himself by working in order to support us. I had the easiest sacrifice, that of myself as channel. The contact was hard on me, and I wasted away under the brilliant energy of Ra's vibration, losing two to three pounds per session. But I would gladly have died in this service, for during these sessions, Don was a happy man. This was the only time during which I knew him that he was not melancholy in his quiet way. To see him fulfilled and content was one of the greatest sources of pleasure in my whole life, for I knew that I'd been a part of that. It was worth everything, and I'd do it all again in a heartbeat, even the extremities of grief that we all felt as Donald sickened and perished, and I came closer and closer to death through the years following Don's suicide. My part of sacrifice has been turned into joy and satisfaction, and I know Don and Jim feel the same.

That reviewer at the agency was quite right to view the language of Ra as technical. It represents the most balanced attempt I have ever read at creating a vocabulary for talking about metaphysical issues with neutral emotional words. It may be stilted at first read, but one always knows what Ra is trying to say, a real achievement in such subjects.

Session 37,
March 12, 1981

QUESTIONER: Is Ra familiar with the results of our efforts today to publish the first book that we did?

RA: I am Ra. This is correct.

QUESTIONER: I don't know if you can comment on the difficulty that we will have in making the Law of One available to those who would require it and want it. It is not something that is easy to disseminate to those who want it at this time. I am sure that there are many, especially the Wanderers, who want this information, but we will have to do something else in order to get it into their hands in the way of added material, I am afraid. Is it possible for you to comment on this?

RA: I am Ra. It is possible.

QUESTIONER: Will you comment on it?

RA: I am Ra. We shall. Firstly, the choosing of this group to do some work to serve others was of an intensive nature. Each present sacrificed much for no tangible result. Each may search its heart for the type of sacrifice, knowing that the material sacrifices are the least; the intensive commitment to blending into an harmonious group at the apex of sacrifice.

Under these conditions, we found your vibration. We observed your vibration. It will not be seen often. We do not wish to puff up the pride, but we shall not chaffer with the circumstances necessary for our particular contact. Thus you have received and we willingly undertake the honor/duty of continuing to offer transmissions of concepts which are, to the best of our abilities, precise in nature and grounded in the attempt to unify many of those things that concern you.

Secondly, the use you make of these transmissions is completely at your discretion. We suggest the flowing of the natural intuitive senses and a minimum of the distortion towards concern. We are content, as we have said, to be able to aid in the evolution of one of your peoples. Whatever effort you make cannot disappoint us, for that number already exceeds one.

QUESTIONER: I have been very hesitant to ask certain questions for fear that they would be regarded, as I regard them, as questions of unimportance or of too great a specificity and thereby reduce our contact with you. In order to disseminate some of the information that I consider to be of great importance—that is, the nontransient type of information, information having to do with the evolution of mind, body, and spirit, it seems almost necessary in our society to include information that is of little value simply because that is how our society works, how the system of distribution appraises that which is offered for distribution. Will you comment on this problem that I have?

RA: I am Ra. We comment as follows: It is quite precisely correct that the level and purity of this contact is dependent upon the level and purity of information sought. Thusly, the continued request for specific information from this particular source is deleterious to the substance of your purpose. Moreover, as we scanned your mind to grasp your situation as regards the typescript of some of our words, we found that you had been criticized for the type of language construction used to convey data. Due to our orientation with regard to data, even the most specifically answered question would be worded by our group in such a way as to maximize the accuracy of the nuances of the answer. This, however, mitigates against what your critic desires in the way of simple, lucid prose. More than this we cannot say. These are our observations of your situation. What you wish to do is completely your decision, and we remain at your service in whatever way we may be without breaking the Way of Confusion.

QUESTIONER: We will attempt to work around these problems in the dissemination of the Law of One. It will take some careful work to do this. I personally will not cease while still incarnate to disseminate this. It will be necessary to write a book, probably about UFOs, because the Law of One is connected with the phenomenon. It's connected with all phenomena, but this seems to be the easiest entry for dissemination. I plan firstly to use the UFO in the advertising sense, as it was meant by the Confederation as an entry into an explanation of the process of evolution that is going on on this planet, and how the rest of the Confederation has been involved in a more understandable way, shall I say, for the population that will read the book. We will use the Ra material in undistorted form, just as it has been recorded here in various places throughout the book, to amplify and clarify what we are saying in the book. This is the only way that I can see right now to create enough dissemination for the people who would like to have the Law of One for them to be able to get it. I could just print up the material that we have off of the tape recorder and publish it, but we wouldn't be able to disseminate it very well because of distribution problems. Will you comment on my second idea of doing a general book on UFOs, including the material from the Law of One?

RA: I am Ra. We shall comment. We hope that your Ra plans materialize. This is a cosmic joke. You were asking for such an example of humor, and we feel this is a rather appropriate nexus in which one may be inserted. Continue with your intentions to the best of your natures and abilities. What more can be done, my friends?

Fragment 23

Serving as the instrument for the Ra contact was very wearing on Carla. She would lose between two and three pounds per session, and the psychic-greeting component of the contact often intensified her arthritic distortions to the point that her functioning on all levels was severely curtailed. Thus, Don and I had hoped that one or the other of us could take her place from time to time in order to give her rest, but neither of us was properly prepared for this service. So rest was obtained by spacing the sessions out over a greater period of time, and we all contented ourselves with the fact that there was a price to be paid for being able to offer this kind of service, and Carla would have to bear the brunt of that price.

I cannot express the amount of pleasure I felt at being able to serve in this way. To see Donald happy and inspired was a satisfaction of the heart that struck to the depths of my being. I adored Don and wished to make him comfortable and happy. But he was not comfortable in this world and so often felt painfully lonely and isolated, although this was never mentioned, nor did he show it in any way. For some reason, his pain and loneliness were always utterly apparent to me and called forth my deepest sympathy and desire to nurture. The days of the Ra contact were golden indeed. I would have died quite gladly doing one last session, and rather expected to, and embraced that freely, but Don's death came first. So I remain! The years since his death have opened to me a wonderful path of service, as readers write in, and I have become counselor and friend to so many all over the world. It is as though I received a second life, for truly when Donald died, the Carla that was, was gone. He had taken a 25-year-old and molded her to his needs, with my willing aid. I became truly his creature. When I woke up from that life, 16 years later, I was neither that 25-year-old nor Don's. I really had to start from scratch to discover my current self.

Session 38, March 13, 1981

QUESTIONER: Will you tell us if there would be any hope or any purpose in either Jim or me taking the instrument's place as instrument by attempting the trance work ourselves?

RA: I am Ra. This information is on the borderline of infringement upon free will. We shall, however, assume your desire to constitute permission to speak slightly beyond limits set by Confederation guidelines, shall we say.

At this space/time nexus, neither the one known as Don nor the one known as Jim is available for this working. The one known as Don, by, shall we say, practicing the mechanics of contact and service to others by means of the channeling, as you call it, would in a certain length of your time become able to do this working. The one known as Jim would find it difficult to become a channel of this type without more practice also over a longer period of time. Then we should have to experiment with the harmonics developed by this practice. This is true in both cases.

Fragment 24
The difficulties in recovering physical energy that Carla experienced as a result of the two experiences with LSD continued to shorten sessions and keep her condition somewhat fragile. We again saw not only the powerful effects of this chemical agent—which we do not recommend to anyone—but the even more powerful effects of unwise choices made by those who wish above all else to be of service to others. As time and experience with the Ra contact accumulated, we became increasingly aware that the honor of providing this kind of service brought with it the need for just as much responsibility for providing the service with as much purity and harmony as one was capable of producing in every

facet of the life experience. What was learned needed to be put to use in the daily life, or difficulties would result in the life pattern that were the means by which the subconscious mind would provide the opportunity to regain the balance and harmony that had been lost. These difficulties could then also be intensified by Orion crusaders in the form of psychic greetings designed to stop the contact with Ra.

We also discovered that every person who incarnates brings with him or her certain avenues, preferences, or ways of nurturing its inner beingness. This inner beingness is that which is the true enabler and ennobler of our daily lives. When we would ask Ra how best to aid the instrument, we would often get more-specific suggestions according to the situation, but we would always be reminded of those qualities that were Carla's ways of nurturing her inner beingness.

Data from the Ra contact indicates that I never had much actual physical energy at all, which fits with my own personal, subjective sense of myself as one who runs on spiritual and mental energy, and as one physically lazy. I call it laziness because I have such a hard time making myself do physical work, unless it is walking and wandering, dancing or swimming, rhythmic activities I love. Even as a young child I was easily able to sit and read, or sit and imagine, for hours. So the sessions we were doing completely exhausted my actual innate physical energy quite quickly. To this very day, I think that since then I have always run on nerve alone, and the simple joy of being alive, which I have in abundance.

Don and Jim both were very upright persons of marked integrity and character, which helped tremendously, as the process of psychic greeting could work only on our inherent distortions. They loved each other and treated each other with great respect, and did their utmost to care for me. They were wonderful in making sure that all was done as well as possible to make me more comfortable. I also had the advantage of being a straight-arrow kind of soul all my life. So the negative energy could only intensify my many physical "problems." Thus the sessions were extremely wearing, but I gloried in them nevertheless, for seeing Don's pleasure in the talks with Ra was more than enough payment to me. I was and am careless of life force if by giving it I can see another live more fully.

I should note that I see the purity that Ra speaks of in myself not as a shining virtue or as a personal achievement, but rather as a gift of nature. I cannot remember a time when I was other than completely involved in the passion of my life: that life itself. I saw myself as a child of God and wanted my life to be a gift to that deity. I was drawn to virtue as others are to gambling or drugs. This inexplicable condition still prevails—my hopes for this life remain simply the giving of all I have to the Creator. What this purity is not is celibacy or retreat from the workings of the world. I have always followed my relationships and based my life around them, trusted my passion, and had an earthy, even vulgar side. I simply find life a wonder and a joy, and all the limitation, mess, loss, and pain in this world have not changed my mind on that.

Session 39,
March 16, 1981

QUESTIONER: The instrument was wondering if the fragile feeling she has now is the result of the chemical ingestion of about six weeks ago.

RA: I am Ra. This is correct. This instrument is now undergoing the most intensive period of physical complex debilitation/distortion due to the doubling effects of the two ingestions. This instrument may expect this extremity to proceed for a period of fifteen to twenty of your diurnal cycles. The weakness distortions will then begin to lift; however, not as rapidly as we first thought due to this instrument's weakness distortions. This instrument is very fortunate in having a support group which impresses upon it the caution necessary as regards these sessions at this time. This instrument is capable of almost instantaneously clearing the mental/emotional complex and the spiritual complex for the purity this working requires, but this instrument's distortion towards fidelity to service does not function to its best use of judgment regarding the weakness distortions of the physical complex. Thus we appreciate your assistance at space/times such as that in your most recent decision-making not to have a working. This was the appropriate decision, and the guidance given this instrument was helpful.

QUESTIONER: Is there anything that the instrument can do in addition to what she is attempting to do to help her condition get better faster? I know that she hasn't been able to exercise because of her foot problem for the last couple of days, but we are hoping to get back to that. Is there anything else that she could do?

RA: I am Ra. As we have implied, the negative entities are moving all stops out to undermine this instrument at this time. This is the cause of the aforementioned problem with the pedal digit. It is fortunate that this instrument shall be greatly involved in the worship of the One Infinite Creator through the vibratory complexes of sacred song during this period. The more active physical existence, both in the movements of exercise and in the sexual sense, are helpful. However, the requirement of this instrument's distortions toward what you would call ethics have an effect upon this latter activity. Again, it is fortunate that this instrument has the opportunities for loving social intercourse, which are of some substantial benefit. Basically, in your third-density continuum, this is a matter of time.

QUESTIONER: From your reading of the instrument's condition, can you approximate how often and the length of workings we should plan on in future workings?

RA: I am Ra. This query borders upon infringement. The information given sets up fairly followable guidelines. However, we are aware that not only can each of you not read this instrument's aura and so see conditions of the physical complex, but also the instrument itself has considerable difficulty penetrating the precise distortion condition of its physical complex due to its constant dependence upon its will to serve. Therefore, we believe we are not infringing if we indicate that one working each alternate diurnal period in the matinal hours is most appropriate, with the possibility of a shorter working upon the free matinal period if deemed appropriate. This is so not only during this period but in general.

Fragment 25
Almost everyone on the path of consciously seeking the truth has had some kind of mystical experience that may or may not make much sense to the person. Most such experiences remain unfathomable to our conscious minds and accomplish their work in an unseen and incomprehensible fashion. Being inhabitants of the third density, with the great veil of forgetting drawn over our ability to see and to truly know, we must content ourselves with the fact that we only make the barest beginnings upon understanding in this illusion. But we may also rest assured that there are no mistakes, and that the events of our lives, whether ordinary or extraordinary, fall into the appropriate place at the appropriate time.

Don had several experiences of altered consciousness that were permanently etched into his mind. The initiation he spoke of here was received in 1968, while we were in meditation together. He suddenly found himself in a world where the colors were living. He said these colors made our earthly hues look like black-and-white photos. They were three-dimensional. He saw living waters, and a golden sunrise streaming over the sky. He could open his eyes and he was in his chair, then close them again and see the other world. This state lasted about half an hour. The other event that is notable, to me, was a night he was meditating and found his arm moving rapidly up and down from elbow to fingers as his arm rested upon the chair arm. A blue light began to emanate from his lower arm, and he was forever grateful that he had company who saw his arm turning blue and glowing. Later transmissions indicated that the UFO entities were winding his battery!

Session 42,
March 22, 1981

QUESTIONER: I had one experience in meditation which I spoke of before which was very profound, approximately twenty years ago, a little less. What disciplines would be most applicable to create this situation and this type of experience?

RA: I am Ra. Your experience would best be approached from the ceremonial magical stance. However, the Wanderer or adept shall have the far-greater potential for this type of experience, which, as you have undoubtedly analyzed to be the case, is one of an archetypal nature, one belonging to the roots of cosmic consciousness.

QUESTIONER: Was that in any way related to the Golden Dawn in ceremonial magic?

RA: I am Ra. The relationship was congruency.

QUESTIONER: Then in attempting to reproduce this experience, would I then best follow the practices for the Order of the Golden Dawn in reproducing this?

RA: I am Ra. To attempt to reproduce an initiatory experience is to move, shall we say, backwards. However, the practice of this form of service to others is appropriate in your case, working with your associates. It is not well for positively polarized entities to work singly. The reasons for this are obvious.

QUESTIONER. Then this experience was a form of initiation? Is this correct?

RA: I am Ra. Yes.

Fragment 26
(Entire session)

Session 44 was removed from Book II because it is almost entirely a maintenance session. In querying as to how best to revitalize Carla's physical vehicle and aid the contact with Ra in general, we did, however, discover a couple of fundamental principles that we found useful thereafter.

In the first answer, we found that a strong desire to be of service is not enough when it is uninformed by wisdom. Carla, and our entire group as well, suffered in the first months of the Ra contact from an overactive desire to be of service through having more sessions with Ra than was helpful for the contact over the long run. Scheduling so many sessions in such a short period of time was overly draining on Carla's physical energy and would mean that the total number of sessions that was possible during her incarnation was probably being reduced.

The second principle that we found of interest was the power of dedication. If Carla dedicated herself to having a session with Ra, she would expend an amount of energy equal to a full day's work—even if the session did not occur. Thus, it was most important that her dedication be informed by wisdom, if not her own then that of the support group's. Thus, for any person, it is the will that drives the dedication, all thoughts, words, and actions depending therefrom. As one points the will, one's desires become manifest. It is important, therefore, that one use the will carefully.

My body has always been fragile. Born with birth defects, laid low by rheumatic fever at the age of 2 years and kidney failure at ages 13 and 15, I have since worked with an increasing amount of rheumatoid arthritis and other rheumatoid diseases. By 1981, when the contact with Ra began, I had had several operations on my wrists and finger joints and was experiencing rheumatoid changes in virtually every joint in my body, the neck and back being the worst hit after the hands. I had worked as a librarian, a job I loved, and as a researcher and writer for Don, but 1976 was the last year I was able to manage a typewriter, and by 1981 I was on Social Security disability and having grave problems physically, both organic and rheumatoid. I was in pain constantly. I tolerated this without much remark and tried to appear well; indeed, I felt healthy. But the body was a weak one. And I think that the trance state was difficult, because without my being able to move my body around, it simply lay in one position during the sessions. This meant that the bad joints were liable to become far more painful, especially in those joints of back, neck, and wrist that were severely damaged. I would wake up in a world of hurt. There did not seem to be a way to avoid this, and it was easy for me to be discouraged at my imperfect physical vehicle. I felt as though I were letting the group down when Ra said they had to limit the session length, and always tried my hardest to maximize my time in trance.

Donald and Jim never reproached me even the first time and were endlessly patient in working with my limitations. However, I cried many a tear of frustration, for I wished so much to be able to continue with this channeling of Ra. It was fortunate for the contact that Jim and I were lovers, for apparently all the physical energy I had to give, after the first few sessions, was the energy transferred during lovemaking. How does a person called "pure" have a lover? Purely, of course. I tried celibacy for about two years when Don and I first got together. I found it extremely difficult and unsatisfying as a life choice. After talking this over with Donald, we agreed that I would take a lover if I wished. As he was gone fully half of the time flying for Eastern Air Lines, I was able to be completely discreet. He never saw the lover, who never saw him. When Jim began coming to meditations regularly, I had once again been celibate for about four years, not having anyone I felt good about to be a lover and friend. Jim was the answer to a maiden's prayers, being extremely fond of his solitude most of the time, but a marvelous companion and an amazing lover when he was in the mood. He wanted nothing from me in the everyday sense of having a constant companion. Don wanted only that companionship. The two men fitted into my life like puzzle pieces, just so. It was, for the time it lasted, a seamless and wonderful threesome of those who truly and entirely wished to serve.

I pondered Ra's words about martyrdom for some time and eventually decided that I should take a vacation, the first one I had taken since 1971. Jim and I went to the seashore, and I rested and felt great healing. I see this as the first step I took away from the forces of death and toward an embrace of continued life. I wish that Don could also have done this, but it was not in him.

I think Ra's comments on how to treat psychic greeting are very wise. To look on these experiences of being "attacked" as less than vitally important was to invite their prolongation. When faced and given full consideration, without fear, just being with these energies and loving them, seeing them as the dark side of oneself, the greetings were simply experiences to have and to ponder, working toward acceptance of the full self. Jesus suggested that we not resist evil, and I think this is part of what He meant—to embrace the greeting as coming from the self, and as loved by the self, was to draw its teeth and neutralize its venom.

Donald had a long-standing interest in ritual magic, one that predated my arrival in his life. He was fascinated with the thought that somehow he could help me by dealing with the negative entities that were offering greetings. It has always been an uneasy thought that he, as he once discussed with Jim, might have tried to make a pact with the entity that was so persistently greeting me, to give himself instead of me.

Session 44 (in total), March 28, 1981

RA: I am Ra. I greet you in the love and in the light of the One Infinite Creator. We communicate now.

QUESTIONER: The instrument had some question as to her vitality. We were having some difficulty in appraising it. Is it possible for you to comment on this?

RA: I am Ra. We scan this instrument and find that we may be of service without infringement due to this instrument's decision to abide by the most careful appraisal possible rather than the most desired.

We have been surprised that we have been able to maintain contact on a regular basis during this most intense period of negatively influenced interference. Sexual-energy transfers have at some workings given this instrument additional vital resources upon which to draw. However, this is not so at this working, and, therefore the will of the instrument drives its bodily complex. This instrument has no judgment about this service. The faculty of will, while recognized as most central and valuable, could in this application cause serious distortion in the bodily complex of the instrument. May we note that martyrdom is not necessarily helpful. We ask this instrument to examine these thoughts, judge, and discriminate the possible truth of them, and if they be deemed true, we suggest this instrument release the power of judgment to the support group, whose interests are balanced far more than this instrument's. Allow decisions to be made without expectation or attachment to the outcome. Our hopes, may we say, for long-term contact through this instrument depend upon its maturing ability to be of service to other-selves by accepting their help and thus remaining a viable instrument.

May we thank the questioner for allowing us to speak to this point, for we were aware of the distortions incumbent upon one whose will to serve is not regulated by knowledge of limitations of bodily complex distortion.

QUESTIONER: Could you please terminate this contact as soon as necessary, since we are not aware of the vitality of the instrument at this time?

RA: I am Ra. In your way of speaking, our hands are, to a certain extent, tied. This instrument has called upon inner reserves which are dearly bought. Therefore, we have the honor/duty of using this energy to the best of our ability. When it becomes low, we shall most certainly, as always, express the need for ending the working. The only way of avoiding this sharing of service at whatever cost is to refrain from the working. It is a dilemma.

QUESTIONER: Can you tell me what the tone was that I heard in my left ear when you started your communication?

RA: I am Ra. This was a negatively oriented signal.

QUESTIONER: Can you tell me how I would hear a positively oriented signal?

RA: I am Ra. Two types there are of positive signal. First, in the right-ear location the signal indicates a sign that you are being given some unworded message saying, "Listen. Take heed." The other positive sign is the tone above the head, which is a balanced confirmation of a thought.

QUESTIONER: Are there any other negatively oriented signals that I get?

RA: I am Ra. This is correct. You are able to receive thought-forms, word-forms, and visions. However, you seem able to discriminate.

QUESTIONER: Is there a reason that I am open to these signals of a negative nature?

RA: I am Ra. Are you not all things?

QUESTIONER: I think that it might be a good idea if we terminated the contact at this time to allow the instrument to gain more of the necessary energy before continuing these sessions. This is my decision at this time. I would very much like to continue the contact, but it seems to me, although I can't tell the instrument's level, that the instrument should not use up any more energy.

RA: I am Ra. We are responding to an unasked query. However, it is most salient and therefore we beg your forgiveness for this infringement. The energy has been lost to the instrument, dedicated to this purpose only. You may do as you will, but this is the nature of the instrument's preparation for contact and is the sole reason we may use it.

QUESTIONER: I am not sure if I fully understood you. Could you say that in a little different way? Could you explain more completely?

RA: I am Ra. Each of you in this working has consciously dedicated the existence now being experienced to service to others. This instrument has refined this dedication through long experience with the channeling, as you term it, of Confederation philosophy, as you may say. Thus when we first contacted this instrument, it had offered its beingness, not only to service to other-selves but service by communication of this nature. As this contact has developed, this dedication of beingness has become quite specific. Thus, once the vital energy is dedicated by the instrument to our communications, even if the working did not occur, this vital energy would be lost to the day-by-day experience of the instrument. Thus we indicated the importance of the instrument's releasing of the will from the process of determining the times of working, for if the instrument desires contact, the energy is gathered and thus lost for ordinary or mundane purposes.

QUESTIONER: In that case, since her energy is already lost, we might as well continue with this session, and we should very carefully monitor the instrument and be the sole judge of when the sessions should occur. Am I correct?

RA: I am Ra. This is profoundly correct. This instrument's determination to continue contact during this period has already extended the low-energy period.

QUESTIONER: This is very revealing to us. Thank you. Each of us gets signals and dreams. I have been aware of clairaudient communication at least once in waking up. Can you suggest a method whereby we might be able, shall I say, to nullify the influence of that which we don't want of a negative source?

RA: I am Ra. There are various methods. We shall offer the most available or simple. To share the difficult contact with the other-selves associated with this working and to meditate in love for these senders of images and light for self and other-selves is the most available means of nullifying the effects of such occurrences. To downgrade these experiences by the use of intellect or the disciplines of will is to invite the prolonging of the effects. Far better, then, to share in trust such experiences and join hearts and souls in love and light with compassion for the sender and armor for the self.

QUESTIONER: Can you tell me the source of the instrument's dream this morning as soon as she woke up?

RA: I am Ra. The feeling of the dream, shall we say, was Orion influenced. The clothing of the dream revealing more the instrument's unconscious associative patterns of symbolism.

QUESTIONER: In meditation a number of years ago, my arm started to glow and to move rapidly involuntarily. What was that?

RA: I am Ra. The phenomenon was an analogy made available to you from your Higher Self. The analogy was that the being that you were was living in a way not understood by, shall we say, physicists, scientists, or doctors.

QUESTIONER: What I am trying to get at in this session is if there are any practices that we might be able to do to best revitalize the instrument, for it is going to be necessary to do all we can in order to maintain our contact. Can you tell us what we can do to increase the instrument's vitality for these contacts?

RA: I am Ra. Your experience was a function of your ability to contact intelligent infinity. Therefore, it does not have a direct bearing upon this instrument's vital energy.

We have spoken before of those things which aid this instrument in the vital energy: the sensitivity to beauty, to the singing of sacred music, to the meditation and worship, to the sharing of self with self in freely given love either in social or sexual intercourse. These things work quite directly upon the vitality. This instrument has a distortion towards appreciation of variety of experiences. This, in a less direct way, aids vitality.

QUESTIONER: I was looking at a diagram of the advancement of magical practices, starting from Malkuth and ending at Kether. I was wondering if these corresponded to the colors or the densities, with Malkuth as one, Yesod as two, Hod and Netzach being three, Tiphareth four, and so on. Is this correct?

RA: I am Ra. This is basically incorrect, although you are upon the correct track of thinking. Each of these stations has a complex number and shading of energy centers, as well as some part in various balances; the lower, the middle, the high, and the total balance. Thus there are complex colors or rays and complex charges, if you will, in each station.

QUESTIONER: Does the left-hand path of this represent the service-to-self path and the right-hand path the service to others?

RA: I am Ra. This will be the last full query of this working.
 This is incorrect. These stations are relationships. Each path has these relationships offered. The intent of the practitioner in working with these powerful concepts determines the polarity of the working. The tools are the tools.

QUESTIONER: As an ending question, I will just ask if it is possible for the Ipsissimus then to have either positive or negative polarity, or must he be neither?

RA: I am Ra. We shall respond to the meaning of this term in a specialized sense. The Ipsissimus is one who has mastered the Tree of Life and has used this mastery for negative polarization.
 Is there any brief query which we may respond to as we take leave of this instrument?

QUESTIONER: I am sorry that we got a little off the track today. I think that the most important thing that we accomplished was discovering how to better regulate the instrument's sessions, and I would hope that you would bear with me for my inability to select questions properly at times. Sometimes I probe into areas to see if it is a direction in which we might go, and, once entering, am then able to determine whether or not to continue in that direction.
 Other than that, all I would like to ask is if there is anything that we can do to make the instrument more comfortable or to improve the contact?

RA: I am Ra. There are no mistakes. Be at rest, my friend. Each of you is most conscientious. All is well. I leave you in the love and the light of the One Infinite Creator. Go forth, therefore, rejoicing in the power and in the peace of the One Infinite Creator. I am Ra. Adonai.

Fragment 27
(Entire session)

Session 45 was also a maintenance session with a few other minor areas of investigation included. The sessions were at their shortest at this time while Carla was regaining her vital energy level. At the end of the session, Ra found the need to end the session somewhat prematurely. The fellows who delivered our water for our cistern had shown up and failed to read our notes on the door, which said that we were not available and that silence was required for the experiment in which we were engaged. Thus they proceeded to knock loudly on every door that they could find, including the door to the Ra session room. Needless to say, we blocked our driveway after that experience so that we would not again be disturbed by visitors while we were having a session with Ra.

This must have been a hilarious situation. I am sorry I missed it. We were so very careful in preparing our place of working, getting the various preparations done with care and grace, then my going off to sleep while Don and Jim walked the circle of One. And then, the exquisitely careful choice of questions, listening for Ra's very soft, very uninflected words—altogether a delicate operation. And then to have loud noises and the hurrying emotions behind them—I can just see the two men going quietly ballistic!

It is hard to read the constant reports of my failing energies, even now, because I remember so well the feelings of frustration and anger that I experienced as I offered myself, poor as I was, for contact. Inside, I felt a strength and power of self that was much different from my physical state, and I wondered why I had chosen such a limited physical body. Why had I not given myself a totally healthy body so I could be a better worker for the Light? And yet I knew, at least intellectually and consciously, that all is perfect, that this was the very best configuration of mind and body and energy balance, that this was precisely where I needed to be. Were I not a mystic and able to access that part of me that is pure faith, I would have been tempted to give up.

In the time since Don's death and the end of the Ra contact, I have come to much more of a peace with this issue, seeing clearly the way my limitations worked to refine me, to hone my sense of purpose and make ever more substantial those joys of spirit that informed my awareness. I see them still at work and can embrace now that fragility, which has given me such fruits of consciousness and hollowed me out so well. It is the empty instrument that is able to offer the purest substance through it, and it is limitation and loss that have refined and hollowed me and given me that transparency of spirit that moves into simple joy. I am so very glad to see each new day—I cannot express it, and this is a gift given through suffering. So often, as we look at spiritual gifts, that is true: the gaining of them can be seen to involve tragedy and pain. Yet, as we experience those depths of sorrow, we also find ourselves more able to move into joy in the everyday things that are so right and so precious.

Session 45 (in total), April 6, 1981

RA: I am Ra. I greet you in the love and in the light of the One Infinite Creator. We communicate now.

QUESTIONER: Could you give us an estimate of the instrument's physical condition now that she is rested?

RA: I am Ra. This instrument's condition as regards the bodily complex is extremely poor. This instrument is not rested. However, this instrument was eager for our contact.

QUESTIONER: Did the period of abstinence from contact help the instrument's physical condition?

RA: I am Ra. This is correct. The probability of this instrument's development of what you would call disease either of the pulmonary nature or the renal nature was quite significant at our previous contact. You have averted a possible serious physical malfunction of this instrument's bodily complex. It is to be noted that your prayerful support was helpful, as was this instrument's unflagging determination to accept that which was best in the long run and thus maintain the exercises recommended without undue impatience. It is to be further noted that those things which aid this instrument are in some ways contradictory and require balance. Thus this instrument is aided by rest but also by diversions of an active nature. This makes it more difficult to aid this instrument. However, once this is known, the balancing may be more easily accomplished.

QUESTIONER: Can you tell me if a large percentage of the Wanderers here now are those of Ra?

RA. I am Ra. I can.

QUESTIONER: Are they?

RA: I am Ra. A significant portion of sixth-density Wanderers are those of our social memory complex. Another large portion consists of those who aided those in South America; another portion, those aiding Atlantis. All are sixth density and all brother and sister groups due to the unified feeling that as we had been aided by shapes such as the pyramid, so we could aid your peoples.

QUESTIONER: Can you say if any of the three of us are of Ra or any of the other groups?

RA: I am Ra. Yes.

QUESTIONER: Can you say which of us are of which group?

RA: I am Ra. No.

QUESTIONER: Are all of us of one of the groups that you mentioned?

RA: I am Ra. We shall go to the limits of our attempts to refrain from infringement. Two are a sixth-density origin, one a fifth-density harvestable to sixth but choosing to return as a Wanderer due to a loving association between teacher and student. Thus you three form a greatly cohesive group.

QUESTIONER: Can you explain the right and left ear tone and what I call touch contact that I continually get?

RA: I am Ra. This has been covered previously. Please ask for specific further details.

QUESTIONER: I get what I consider to be tickling in my right and my left ear at different times. Is this any different as far as meaning goes from the tone that I get in my right and left ear?

RA: I am Ra. No.

QUESTIONER: Why is the left ear of the service-to-self contact, and the right, service to others?

RA: I am Ra. The nature of your physical vehicle is that there is a magnetic field positive and negative in complex patterns about the shells of your vehicle. The left portion of the head region of most entities is, upon the time/space continuum level, of a negative polarity.

QUESTIONER: Can you tell me what is the purpose or philosophy behind the fourth-, fifth-, and sixth-density positive and negative social memory complexes?

RA: I am Ra. The basic purpose of a social memory complex is that of evolution. Beyond a certain point, the evolution of spirit is quite dependent upon the understanding of self and other-self as Creator. This constitutes the basis for social complexes. When brought to maturity, they become social memory complexes. The fourth density and sixth density find these quite necessary. The fifth positive uses social memory in attaining wisdom, though this is done individually. In fifth negative, much is done without aid of others. This is the last query, as this instrument needs to be protected from depletion. Are there brief queries before we close?

QUESTIONER: I just need to know if there is anything that we can do to make the instrument more comfortable or to improve the contact.

RA: I am Ra. All is well, my brothers. [Loud rapping at the door. Water truckers!]

QUESTIONER: What did you say?

RA: I am Ra. All is well, my brothers. I leave you now in the love and in the light of the One Infinite Creator. Go forth, then, rejoicing in the power and the peace of the One Infinite Creator. Adonai.

Fragment 28

In querying about how best to aid two of our cats as they were about to be put under anesthetic at the veterinarian's, and how to reduce any negative influences that might have sought an inroad while the cats were being operated on, we discovered that when the investment of a second-density being has been successful, that second-density being attracts to it the spirit complex. And the presence of the spirit complex makes that being vulnerable to the same psychic-greeting process that any third-density entity may experience, given the appropriate circumstances. The ritual sentences mentioned are taken from the Book of Common Prayer of the Episcopal Church.

When I was a young woman of 17, I thought I wanted a life full of children and home. But life never offered me that. Instead, I was drawn to follow a life of devotion, to Don and to the Creator. Instead of children, I have had the joy of being friend and/or counselor to many courageous and seeking souls. And cats!! Plenty of cats! I cannot remember being without a cat my whole life long! They delight me, and their company is always a pleasure. We relate to them as children, and they soak up a lot of my maternal feelings!

Gandalf was an exceptionally devoted cat. He loved our laps and would retrieve for Don, catching the peppermint candy wrappers that Don tossed and bringing them to deposit in Don's shoe. When he became old and full of years, he was more than ever devoted, and even after he could no longer walk, if I forgot to carry him with me, he would scrape along the floor little by little to come nearer again. Needless to say, we did not forget him often. And he still lives in loving memories.

Session 46,
April 15, 1981

QUESTIONER: The one question that is bothering us, which I got in meditation, may be an inappropriate question, but I feel it is my duty to ask it because it is central to the instrument's mental condition and ours. It has to do with the two cats which we were going to have worked upon today for teeth cleaning and for the removal of the small growth from Gandalf's leg. I got the impression that there might be an inroad there for the Orion group, and I was primarily concerned if there was anything that we could do for protection for these two cats. It may be out of line for me to ask this question, but I feel it my duty to ask it. Would you please give me any information that you can on that subject?

RA: I am Ra. The entity, mind/body/spirit complex, Gandalf, being harvestable third density, is open to the same type of psychic attack to which you yourselves are vulnerable. Therefore, through the mechanism of images and dreams, it is potentially possible for negative concepts to be offered to this mind/body/spirit complex, thus having possible deleterious results. The entity, Fairchild, though harvestable through investment, does not have the vulnerability to attack in as great amount due to a lack of the mind complex activity in the distortion of conscious devotion.

For protection of these entities, we might indicate two possibilities. Firstly, the meditation putting on the armor of light. Secondly, the repetition of short ritual sentences known to this instrument from the establishment which distorts spiritual oneness for this instrument. This instrument's knowledge will suffice. This will aid due to the alerting of many discarnate entities also aware of these ritual sentences.

The meditation is appropriate at the time of the activity on behalf of these entities. The ritual may be repeated with efficacy from this time until the safe return, at convenient intervals.

QUESTIONER: I am not familiar with the ritual sentences. If the instrument is familiar, you need not answer this, but which sentences do you mean?

[*Silence. No response from Ra.*]

QUESTIONER: I assume that the instrument is familiar with them then?

RA: I am Ra. This is correct.

QUESTIONER: Can you tell me something of the little growth on Gandalf's leg, and if it is of danger to him?

RA: I am Ra. The cause of such growths has been previously discussed. The danger to the physical body complex is slight, given the lack of repeated stimulus to anger.

Fragment 29
The spiritual transfer of energy is apparently possible for Carla in any sexual energy transfer. It happens without any particular effort on her part and seems due, primarily, to her nature as one who considers all of her actions, first, in the light of how she may be of service to another. This kind of spiritual energy transfer, however, is possible for anyone to achieve through a conscious mental dedication of the shared sexual intercourse for the purpose of achieving such a transfer. With that dedication consciously made, the male will transfer the physical energy, which he has in abundance, to the female and refresh her, and the female will transfer the mental/emotional and spiritual energies, which she has in abundance, and inspire the male. The kinds of energy transferred by each biological sex are determined by the nature that is unique to each. The biological male tends to express the male principle of that quality that reaches. The biological female tends to express the female principle of that quality that awaits the reaching. The orgasm is the point at which the transfer takes place, although well-mated partners do not necessarily need to experience the orgasm in order to achieve the transfer.

Since these sessions were recorded, I have continued to study the sexual part of red-ray activity, with the hope of finding ways to share the beauty and joy I have found in my sexuality with other people who wish to move into the experience of sacramental sex. More and more, I am convinced that we all have the ability to move into this vibratory level, where intercourse becomes ever more deeply a Holy Eucharist of red ray. I think that this orgasmic energy is pure love, and that as we experience this ecstasy, we are simply knowing the creator's vibration at rest. I suspect that the universe dwells in a state of orgasm, a timeless ecstasy. So much of our culture's training is bent on blunting the power of passion, so that social strictures may be observed, that the spontaneity of the act itself is lost. And the constant bombardment of sexual images in commercials and advertisements of every kind sharpen the desire for more and more: more partners, more unorthodox experiences, more thrills, more novelty.

In contrast to this, there is the red-ray part of self and its natural functions, natural and right and, like all other natural functions, something to fulfill in privacy, and with an eye to grace and purity of form in the doing. Once a man has found the wisdom to fix his desire upon Woman, the Goddess, as incarnate in his mate, and the woman has opened her heart to Man, as incarnate in her mate, there is laid the stage for an ever-deeper practice of this glorious natural sharing of energy. It has been a blessing to me, certainly, as I apparently ran out of energy some years ago—but am still alive and kicking! Thanks in no small part to the truly fine natural functions of one James McCarty, a man most lovingly sensitive to the Goddess within.

Session 48,
April 22, 1981

QUESTIONER: I have a question from the instrument that I will read. "You have suggested several times that sexual energy transfers aid the instrument's vital energy and this contact. It seems that this is not true for all people; that the sexual circuitry and the spiritual circuitry are not the same. Is this instrument an anomaly, or is the positive effect of sexual activity on spiritual energy normal for all third-density beings?"

RA: I am Ra. This instrument, though not anomalous, is somewhat less distorted towards the separation of mind, body, and spirit than many of your third-density entities. The energies of sexual transfer would, if run through the undeveloped spiritual electrical or magnetic complex which you call circuitry, effectually blow out that particular circuit. Contrarily, the full spiritual energies run through bodily complex circuitry will also adversely affect the undeveloped circuit of the bodily complex. Some there are, such as this instrument, who have not in the particular incarnation chosen at any time to express sexual energy through the bodily circuitry. Thus, from the beginning of such an entity's experience, the body and spirit express together in any sexual action. Therefore, to transfer sexual energy for this instrument is to transfer spiritually as well as physically. This instrument's magnetic field, if scrutinized by one sensitive, will show these unusual configurations. This is not unique to one entity but is common to a reasonable number of entities who, having lost the desire for orange- and yellow-ray sexual experiences, have strengthened the combined circuitry of spirit, mind, and body to express the totality of beingness in each action. It is for this reason also that the social intercourse and companionship is very beneficial to this instrument, it being sensitive to the more subtle energy transfers.

Fragment 30

I was the one of the three of us most interested in querying about my own experiences. Having once also been a conspiracy buff, this may be understandable as the result of an over-active and over-dramatic curiosity. Questions about Carla were always of a maintenance nature, trying to figure out the best way to keep her physical vehicle running smoothly or at least running in some cases, and Don seldom queried about himself at all. The following comments by Ra amplify the sacramental function that sexual intercourse can fulfill in one's journey of seeking the truth. With the proper balance of mind and body, uniquely determined for each entity, the orgasm can serve as a kind of triggering mechanism that activates the spirit complex and serves as a kind of shuttle, and which then can allow the entity to contact what Ra calls intelligent infinity.

The "pertinent information" concerning the frontal-lobe portion of the brain that Ra speaks of concerns the fact that no one knows for sure what that part of the brain is for. All of the qualities that make us human beings are accounted for in the rear five-eighths of the reptilian and mammalian brain. Pioneer thinkers studying this portion of the brain have posited the possibility that the frontal lobes are dormant in most people and may be activated by removing the various blockages in the lower energy centers that childhood experiences have placed there, in accordance with pre-incarnative choices of lessons for the incarnation. When these blockages have been removed—i.e., lessons have been learned—then the frontal lobes may in some degree be activated and a quantum leap in consciousness may be experienced for various lengths of time, usually quite short except in the cases of genuine yogis, saints, and mystics. This is the theory. However, Jim is still "looking forward," shall we say.

Jim's fascination, early on, about possible conspiracies of political, economic, and metaphysical nature was one he had in common with a large number of people interested in UFOs and UFO messages. Somehow, the mind that revolved around to the mystery of UFOs was also vulnerable to the sensational and elaborate theories that involved secret governmental and international corporate powers. When I first began to channel in 1974, such questions were very common. It took me several years of experience in channeling and watching how the group energy felt to me, to determine to my own satisfaction that asking questions about this sort of fear-based specific material was substantially detrimental to the tuning of the contact, and therefore to the virtue of the information received. In recent years, I allow and even welcome questions that may touch on specific issues for a questioner—but I also offer caveat that the answer will not be specific. I value highly the good contact we continue to be able to sustain, and guard its tuning carefully.

Jim's whole experience with frontal-lobe research was a life-changing thing. It seemed to be the thing that opened up for him the lifestyle of homesteader, certainly an unusually retiring and abstemious way of life, but one that suited Jim to a tee. So without understanding much of the research, I can see that it was very helpful to Jim. The man who created and promulgated this research, however, was a person increasingly devoted to specific questions, when his students began channeling. So I think Jim learned the hard way that any channel can be tainted when the questioning gets too specific and focuses on worldly things rather than eternal values.

Session 49,
April 27, 1981

QUESTIONER: I have a question here from Jim first. He says: "For the past nine years I have had what I call frontal-lobes experiences in the preconscious state of sleep when I wake up in the morning. They are a combination of pleasure and pressure which begins in the frontal lobes and spreads in pulses through the whole brain and feels like an orgasm in the brain. I have had over 200 of these experiences, and often they are accompanied by voices and visions, which seldom make much sense to me. What is the source of these frontal-lobes experiences?"

RA: I am Ra. We scan the questioner and find some pertinent information already available which regards the physiological disposition of this particular part of the brain. The experiences described and experienced are those distillations which may be experienced after a concentration of effort upon the opening of the gateway or indigo mind complex so that experience of a sacramental or violet ray may occur. These experiences are the beginnings of that which, as the body, the mind, and the spirit become integrated at the gateway or indigo level, may then yield not only the experience of joy but the comprehension of intelligent infinity which accompanies it. Thus the body complex orgasm and mind complex orgasm becoming integrated may then set forth the proper gateway for the spiritual complex integration and its use as a shuttle for the sacrament of the fully experienced presence of the One Infinite Creator. Thus there is much to which the questioner may look forward.

Fragment 31

When I was in the process of cutting trees with which to build my cabin in the woods of central Kentucky in the spring of 1973, I was quite unsure of how or if I would be able to survive alone in that remote environment. Though subdued most of the time, my nervousness about this whole project was obvious. One night, in my tent, I was awakened by the sound of a friend's dog eating dog food from its plastic bowl. I mentally heard the message that is spoken of in the following material and wrote it down by flashlight. It appears that each of us has at least three guides to aid us, and aid is usually given in a symbolic manner in order to give us clues that will stimulate our own thinking and seeking abilities rather than by laying out answers in a plain and unquestionable fashion.

I have experienced Jim's nervousness through our long association and found that his quickness and alertness are preternatural. The trait seems to be a mixed blessing, however, for if the objects he is manipulating have the temerity to be balky, the tension can escalate. I suppose virtues always have their shadows! I have come to find that level of trust with Jim where one accepts another without regard for anything but complete support, and would not change him to be one iota less fiery. That racehorse temperament is simply the shadow of so many wonderful traits that make him the extremely efficient and ever-resourceful good judge of men and situations that he is.

Session 50,
May 6, 1981

QUESTIONER: I have a question from Jim about an experience which he had when he first moved to his land, in which he was told, "The key to your survival comes indirect, through nervousness." The entity was Angelica. Could you give him information with respect to this?

RA: I am Ra. Yes.

QUESTIONER: Would you please do that?

RA: I am Ra. As we have noted, each mind/body/spirit complex has several guides available to it. The persona of two of these guides is the polarity of male and female. The third is androgynous and represents a more unified conceptualization faculty.

The guide speaking as sound vibration complex, Angelica, was the female polarized persona. The message may not be fully explicated due to the Law of Confusion. We may suggest that in order to progress, a state of some dissatisfaction will be present, thus giving the entity the stimulus for further seeking. This dissatisfaction, nervousness, or angst, if you will, is not of itself useful. Thus its use is indirect.

Fragment 32
We have omitted the name of the person contacted in this query in Session 53 because we still would not want to be part of reducing the polarity of those of Ra. We would, however, like to share the rest of the question and answer because it seems to us to be a good illustration of the general principles that extraterrestrials of the positive polarity utilize in their face-to-face encounters with the population of our planet.

In the spring of 1981 Don traveled by himself to Laramie, Wyoming, to give a talk on the Law of One at one of Leo Sprinkle's UFO contactee conferences. The cause of his sickness during that conference and the aid of a support group are interesting points gleaned from that experience. Again, we see the desire not to abridge free will paramount in Ra's answer. The answer was possible because Don had already reached the same general conclusion in his own thinking.

The last question and answer in this section give an interesting perspective on the phenomenon of ball lightning. When Carla was a small child, a ball of what looked to be lightning came in through the window, rolled around her crib, and left through the same window.

When Don was a young child, he had a similar experience.

It would seem that once any seeker dedicates herself to following the path toward the Creator that has opened before her awakening gaze, odd coincidences and events mount up rapidly. The silver flecks were first noticed by Andrija Puharich, as he and Uri Geller worked together. They might be strewn around a hotel room's rug, showing up overnight. After Don and I made contact with Puharich in 1974 and began working with him from time to time, I began getting them on my face and upper body. We got glitter of all the kinds we could find and compared them. The sparkles on my face were not the shape of any of the manufactured kinds. When the contact with those of Ra began, silver flecks started showing up much more frequently. This little phenomenon ended when Donald died in 1984. However, we do continue to be blessed frequently with Ra's other form of saying hello: the hawk. We actually have a family of hawks nesting in our trees for the second year! And often, when Jim and I are discussing something, we will get a hawk sighting just when we come to a decision. It always feels great to see this sign of Love.

Everyone will have his own set of these little signals that say "you are on the beam" or "perhaps not." As illogical as this sounds, we encourage you to note these coincidences when they begin to repeat. They are a definite form of communication with spirit energies that are benign and loving, as far as we can tell.

Our association with Leo Sprinkle is long standing. This courageous researcher became interested in UFO phenomena when asked to participate as hypnotist in the research being done on a UFO contactee. He worked with many such contactees through the years and eventually founded a research organization that holds a yearly Rocky Mountain Conference for UFO contactees. It is a good support group for these witnesses to the unusual. In 1975, we spent a hilarious weekend at a UFO convention held in Fort Smith, Arkansas, working on a movie together. (The movie, The Force Beyond, *turned out so badly that Don renamed it* The Farce Beyond!*) Leo was hypnotizing a UFO witness, Don and I were consultants on the script, and he obtained most of the psychics and witnesses that were in the film. When Leo did the actual hypnosis, things went wrong repeatedly with equipment and so forth, and it was midnight before we sat down to eat. I asked him how he was holding up. Completely deadpan, he dropped his head on the table in front of him as though pole-axed. It was a delightful moment after a long day.*

Since Don and I began talking about these experiences with light coming to greet us, seemingly, we have heard from many others to whom this has also occurred. It is a marvelous thing to ponder. Are these the bodies we shall use to experience a higher density? They are most fair and pure.

Session 53,
May 25, 1981

QUESTIONER: First I will ask if you could tell me the affiliation of the entities who contacted [name].

RA: I am Ra. This query is marginal. We will make the concession towards information with some loss of polarity due to free will being abridged. We request that questions of this nature be kept to a minimum.

The entities in this and some other vividly remembered cases are those who, feeling the need to plant Confederation imagery in such a way as not to abrogate free will, use the symbols of death, resurrection, love, and peace as a means of creating, upon the thought level, the time/space illusion of a systematic train of events which give the message of love and hope. This type of contact is chosen by careful consideration of Confederation members which are contacting an entity of like home vibration, if you will. This project then goes before the Council of Saturn and, if approved, is completed. The characteristics of this type of contact include the nonpainful nature of thoughts experienced and the message content which speaks not of doom but of the new dawning age.

QUESTIONER: It is not necessary that I include the information that you just gave in the book to accomplish my purpose. In order to save your polarity, shall we say, I can keep that as private material if you wish. Do you wish for me to keep it unpublished?

RA: I am Ra. That which we offer you is freely given and subject only to your discretion.

QUESTIONER: I thought you would say that. In that case, can you tell me anything of the "blue book" mentioned by [name] in that case?

RA: I am Ra. No.

QUESTIONER: Can you tell me why [name] has so many silver flecks on her?

RA: I am Ra. This is infringement. No.

QUESTIONER: Thank you. Can you tell me why I got sick during Carl Rushkey's talk?

RA: I am Ra. We scan your thoughts. They are correct, and therefore we do not infringe by confirming them. The space/time of your allotted speaking was drawing near, and you came under Orion attack due to the great desire of some positively oriented entities to become aware of the Law of One. This may be expected, especially when you are not in a group lending strength to each other.

QUESTIONER: Thank you. Can you comment on my and the instrument's, if she approves, so-called ball-of-lightning experiences as a child?

RA: I am Ra. This will be the last query of this working.
You were being visited by your people to be wished well.

Fragment 33

When it becomes known to a seeker that there are negative entities of an unseen nature that may present one with psychic greetings that, in general, tend to intensify difficulties that the seeker has freely chosen, it is often easy for the seeker totally to blame the negative entities for difficulties that appear in the life pattern, rather than continuing to trace the line of responsibility to its source within the free-will choices of the self. I illustrated this trait in the following question.

I had known very well from an early age that I had a well-exercised temper. In Ra's response to my question about that temper, it is interesting to see one possible source for such anger and the potential for balancing that such anger can provide. A future query in this same general area elicits another facet of this quality of anger.

When one feels she has a fault, it is very easy to focus on eliminating the fault. Yet, Ra encourages us not to erase faults but to balance them. I think this to be a key concept. All of us dwelling in this veil of flesh have biases and opinions that seem distorted to some degree. Of course, if one has a fault that involves infringing on the free will of another, then the fault does need to be addressed by eliminating that behavior. One does not find ways to balance thieving or murder. But Jim's anger, my eternal vagueness and forgetfulness, all of people's little quirks, can be seen to be energies that need balancing, rather than removal. One tries to behave completely without error, yet errors occur. This should not be an excuse for the self to judge the self, but rather a chance for the self to offer love and support to the self, while gently bringing the behavior into balance. Unless we get this principle solidly under our metaphysical belts, we will be self-judgmental people who are petty in complaint and grudging with praise, not just for the self, but for others.

Session 59,
June 25, 1981

QUESTIONER: I have a question from Jim, and it states: "I think that I have penetrated my lifelong mystery of my anger at making mistakes. I think that I have always been aware subconsciously of my ability to master new learning, but my desire to successfully complete my work on Earth has been energized by the Orion group into irrational and destructive anger when I fail. Could you comment on this observation?

RA: I am Ra. We would suggest that as this entity is aware of its position as a Wanderer, it may also consider what pre-incarnative decisions it undertook to make regarding the personal or self-oriented portion of the choosing to be here at this particular time/space. This entity is aware, as stated, that it has great potential, but potential for what? This is the pre-incarnative question. The work of sixth density is to unify wisdom and compassion. This entity abounds in wisdom. The compassion it is desirous of balancing has, as its antithesis, lack of compassion. In the more conscious being, this expresses or manifests itself as lack of compassion for self. We feel this is the sum of suggested concepts for thought which we may offer at this time without infringement.

Fragment 34

The first two questions in this portion of Session 60 touch upon Carla's tendency toward martyrdom in general terms; that is, in the case of the Ra contact Carla's desire to be of service in this contact was strong enough that she would open herself completely to the contact until there was no vital energy left for her own ease of transition back to the waking state. Ra's suggestion in this regard was that if she were to reserve some vital energy, it would be possible that the contact could continue over a longer period of time. Ra recognized that her basic incarnational lesson was to generate as much compassion as possible and was the root of the unreserved opening to the contact, but Ra also suggested that a little addition of wisdom in the reserving some small amount of vital energy might enhance her service.

    In fact, our entire group was then in the process of exercising more caution regarding the frequency of sessions. We had begun to travel the martyr's path in having sessions too frequently and giving of the self—of the instrument—until there was nothing left. As we continued to hold sessions when she was not in good shape, it was also suggested to us by Ra that overly to stress caution in scheduling sessions further apart and in resting Carla was as deleterious to retaining the contact as our martyring behavior was at the beginning of the sessions. In having the sessions, in distributing the material to others, and in living the daily life in general, we found that there is a basic kind of dedication to serving others that is helpful. But when that dedication becomes focused on a strong desire that a specific outcome be the result of any effort to serve others, then one is distorting the service with preconceived ideas. "Not my will, but Thy will" is the attitude offering the most-efficient service.

And once again we see the beneficial role that a physical limitation can play in one's incarnation. In this case, Carla's arthritis is seen to be the means by which she pre-incarnatively determined to focus her attention, not on the usual activities of the world but on the inner life, the life of meditation and contemplation that her physical limitation offered her. This same limitation has also been used to carry out other pre-incarnatively chosen lessons, as mentioned by Ra in the last two responses. Such pre-incarnatively chosen limitations confound many healers, who have the opinion that no disease is ever necessary. However, it seems that some people choose lessons that will utilize the entire incarnation and not just a portion of it. Thus, the distortions needed to present the opportunities for these kinds of lessons are not meant to yield to healing efforts.

It may seem as though I have had a life ruled by disease and limitation. In actuality, that just isn't so. At one time, when Donald had died and I had not yet fully decided to survive him, my condition worsened to the point where I had to stay horizontal all the time. But even then, I was able to make letter tapes and to channel, until the very end of that dark period, the month or so before going to the hospital in January 1992. And I can honestly say that even in that extremity, I wanted to stay.

Today, I simply do not think very much about my aches and pains, and I don't think other people notice anything out of the ordinary about me. I don't appear ill and do not act that way either, so people just assume I am healthy. Having done everything I could to better my condition, and failed to make any dent by any means, I have concluded that the symptoms of pain that I experience are not signal, but noise. This is the basic pain management theory I learned in rehab that fateful year of 1992. Something that has no message is a useless thing, no matter how irritating. I was riding one of those electric buggies airline employees use to transport the elderly and feeble, and remarked on the constant bee-baw, bee-baw, bee-baw as the cart wended its way through the pedestrian traffic in the huge corridor. The driver said she didn't even notice it any more, she was so used to it. Exactly.

I don't do this perfectly: I complain at least daily to my mate, who has identified listening to the daily report as a service to the weary! It really helps to gripe a bit. As long as the griper doesn't take it too seriously.

I know this is not easy, and I spent months during that period thinking that I might not make the cut! It is difficult to face pain, especially ancient, blade-keen pain that has crippled, and to work through the crystallizations that kept the arms down and the back separated from the neck. What saved me was love. I have a real passion for cooking. I love to play with tastes, to mix herbs and spices and all the kinds of food there are. The fact that the result of this playtime is meals that people enjoy is icing on the cake! I'd been banned from the kitchen twelve years ago. After thorough testing to be sure I would not harm my condition, I was OK'd to take up cooking again. I loved being in the kitchen, to the point where I would just hang on to the stove and cook long past the point where I would have given up if I'd just been sitting or standing and doing nothing. And then there was the love I had for Jesus—I promised Him that I would get better, and give praise and thanksgiving and glory to His holy Name. Which I do, frequently! Between the two, a miracle occurred for me, given by Love to love for Love's sake. And I pray to be able to share my story of being a Wanderer and one who wishes to serve, with all those who are awakening to their spiritual identity at this time.

Yes, I am still limited by my physical restrictions. I have spent literally years refining a schedule that I can live with, that has the most things in it that I want in my life, without over-stressing my frail body. At this point, Jim and I have things worked out very well, and I have been fortunate to escape difficulty this last year or so. It is a first! I just take things at the speed I know is safe for me.

Needless to say, when this contact was ongoing, I had no such concept of caution. I adored Don—he wanted this contact more than anything I'd ever seen him go after; during this time he was actually a happy man. These were golden moments for me: I had had but one goal for a long time from 1968 onward, and that was to make a real home, both physical and metaphysical, for Don. I knew he was comforted by being with me, so I felt I always helped. But this state he was in was unique. Here was my star-crossed love, peaceful and completely satisfied with his life for the first and only time I ever saw. I couldn't wait to do the next session, just so I could wake up to see him grinning with delight.

It is fairly easy to see from the questions he was asking that Don felt my best chance for healing lay in mental work along the lines of his Church of Christ Scientist mother's faith. He was accustomed, when a family member got a cold or illness, to calling the practitioner, who would spend time in prayer and meditation, affirming the perfection of whatever seemed to be imperfect. This method of thinking is extremely valuable, and I do want to give credit to this marvelous practice of affirming perfection. For that is the over-riding truth—behind all of this seeming imperfection there is utter perfection beyond telling or measure. I have sensed and felt it but have never been able to bring back words. However, I believe those experiences to be true.

As to the idea of my pre-incarnatively choosing the limitations and the lesson of loving without expectation of a return, both of these topics had been covered in a past-life regression done by Larry Allison in 1975, and I felt sure that this was the case. It rang true with that depth of resonance I have come to associate with personal truth. I felt and feel fortunate to be alive, and if I have to pay some dues, that's OK. I'm glad to be at the party! When I do die to this world, I hope that I will be satisfied I've done all I can—and I don't feel that way yet. One thing I know I still have ahead is to write some sort of witness to those truths that have been shared with me at dear cost. When I have written all I know about the devotional life lived in the midst of it all, then I will be fairly satisfied that I have served my part. But we never really know what the sum of service is, do we? I don't presume to think that I know all that is slated for me to experience. And am satisfied to let it surprise me.

Session 60,
July 1, 1981

QUESTIONER: It is my opinion that the best way for the instrument to improve her condition is through periods of meditation followed by periods of contemplation with respect to the condition and its improvement. Could you tell me if I am correct, and expand on this?

RA: I am Ra. Meditation and contemplation are never untoward activities. However, this activity will in all probability, in our opinion, not significantly alter the predispositions of this instrument which cause the fundamental distortions which we, as well as you, have found disconcerting.

QUESTIONER: Can you tell me the best approach for altering, to a more acceptable condition, the distortions that the instrument is experiencing?

RA: I am Ra. There is some small amount of work which the instrument may do concerning its pre-incarnative decisions regarding service to the Infinite Creator in this experience. However, the decision to open without reservation to the offering of self when service is perceived is such a fundamental choice that it is not open to significant alteration, nor would we wish to interfere with the balancing process which is taking place with this particular entity. The wisdom and compassion being so balanced by this recapitulation of fourth density is helpful to this particular mind/body/spirit complex. It is not an entity much given to quibbling with the purity with which it carries out that which it feels it is best to do. We may say this due to the instrument's knowledge of its self, which is clear upon this point. However, this very discussion may give rise to a slightly less fully unstopped dedication to service in any one working, so that the service may be continued over a greater period of your space/time.

QUESTIONER: You are saying, then, that the physical distortions that the instrument experiences are part of a balancing process? Is this correct?

RA: I am Ra. This is incorrect. The physical distortions are a result of the instrument's not accepting fully the limitations placed prior to incarnation upon the activities of the entity once it had begun the working. The distortions caused by this working, which are inevitable given the plan chosen by this entity, are limitation and to a degree consonant with the amount of vital and physical energy expended, weariness, due to that which is the equivalent in this instrument of many, many hours of harsh physical labor.

This is why we suggested the instrument's thoughts dwelling upon the possibility of its suggesting to its Higher Self the possibility of some slight reservation of energy at a working. This instrument at this time is quite open until all resources are quite exhausted. This is well if desired. However, it will, shall we say, shorten the number of workings in what you may call the long run.

QUESTIONER: Will spreading the workings out over greater intervals of time so that we have more time between workings help?

RA: I am Ra. This you have already done. It is not helpful to your group to become unbalanced by concern for one portion of the work above another. If this instrument is, in your judgment, capable, and if the support group is functioning well, if all is harmonious and if the questions to be asked have been considered well, the working is well begun. To overly stress the condition of the instrument is as deleterious to the efficiency of this contact as the antithetical behavior was in your past.

QUESTIONER: Aside from the workings, I am concerned about the physical distortions of the instrument in the area of her hands and arms. Is there a, shall we say, mental exercise or something else that the instrument could work on to help to alleviate the extreme problems that she has at this time with her hands, etc.?

RA: I am Ra. Yes.

QUESTIONER: Would this be an exercise of meditation and contemplation upon the alleviation of these problems?

RA: I am Ra. No.

QUESTIONER: What would she do then, in order to alleviate these problems?

RA: I am Ra. As we have said, this instrument, feeling that it lacked compassion to balance wisdom, chose an incarnative experience whereby it was of necessity placed in situations of accepting self in the absence of other-selves' acceptance and the acceptance of other-self without expecting a return or energy transfer. This is not an easy program for an incarnation but was deemed proper by this entity. This entity therefore must needs meditate and consciously, moment by moment, accept the self in its limitations, which have been placed for the very purpose of bringing this entity to the precise tuning we are using. Further, having learned to radiate acceptance and love without expecting return, this entity now must balance this by learning to accept the gifts of love and acceptance of others which this instrument feels some discomfort in accepting. These two balanced workings will aid this entity in the release from the distortion called pain. The limitations are, to a great extent, fixed.

QUESTIONER: Is the fact that the instrument was already consciously aware of this the reason that the first distortion was not in force in making it impossible for you to communicate this to us?

RA: I am Ra. This is not only correct for this entity, which has been consciously aware of these learn/teachings for some of your years, but also true of each of the support group. The possibility of some of this information being offered was not there until this session.

Fragment 35

Carla's arthritis began just after her kidneys failed when she was thirteen years old. In her childhood she had the very strong desire to be of service to others, but after many difficult experiences as a child unable to fit well anywhere, she felt so sure that she would never be able to really be of service that by the age of thirteen she prayed that she might die. When her kidney failure six months later provided her with an avenue for such an exit from the incarnation, her near-death experience was of the nature where she was told that she could go on if she chose to, but that her work was not done. She immediately chose to return to this life, now feeling that there was indeed service to be provided, and the juvenile rheumatoid arthritis set in immediately.

You can also see here how the efforts of negative entities intensified the choice to die that she had made of free will, but by that same free will there was no force that could hinder her return to service once she had made that choice.

The concept of limitation, especially in the form of physical disease, being a benign thing can be disturbing to think upon at first. I asked myself why in heaven's name would I choose this particular condition? For it is as cunning in how it limits me as it could be. Although the rheumatoid disease has altered each joint in my body, it has focused on my hands, wrists, and shoulders and back. I simply cannot do anything physical for too long a period, including typing at this very computer's keyboard. I cannot pick up heavy things or do heavy cleaning around the house. In general, I must watch how long I work at anything, for I cannot do a good day's work and expect to rise the next day feeling well. I simply must write a lot of rest into the schedule. Any time I do overstep these unseen limitations, I reap the reward of having lots of quiet time while I recuperate.

Through the years, therefore, I have become very able to live in a world that is retired to the point of being a hermit's way. Even in the depths of illness, in the early '90s, I was still given work to do, in the channeling and in correspondence with a wide variety of students, counselees, and friends. My voice, because it hurt to produce a tone, was faint, but my thoughts still flew with wings, and there was immense satisfaction in continuing to serve.

It has always been difficult for me to take things lightly. I am always the one so intensely riveted on whatever I am doing that there's no possibility of my being "cool." Forget it! So Ra's telling me I needed to reserve energy for myself during sessions did not sit well. However, given the way I was physically wasting away, I realized I would have to learn how to do that. I have come to appreciate this lesson greatly and so pass the advice on to each who sees himself in these words. It is a worthwhile thing to preserve the physical shell; indeed, it is the kind of loving act that teaches as it aids.

Session 63, July 18, 1981

QUESTIONER: Was the original problem with the kidneys some twenty-five years ago caused by psychic attack?

RA: I am Ra. This is only partially correct. There were psychic-attack components to the death of this body at that space/time. However, the guiding vibratory complex in this event was the will of the instrument. This instrument desired to leave this plane of existence, as it did not feel it could be of service.

QUESTIONER: You are saying then that the instrument itself created the kidney problem at that time?

RA: I am Ra. The instrument's desire to leave this density lowered the defenses of an already predisposed weak body complex, and an allergic reaction was so intensified as to cause the complications which distorted the body complex towards unviability. The will of the instrument, when it found that there was indeed work to be done in service, was again the guiding factor or complex of vibratory patterns which kept the body complex from surrendering to dissolution of the ties which cause the vitality of life.

Fragment 36

The following material returns to the realm of transient information in general—and a portion of the conspiracy theory specifically—as an outgrowth of our querying about prophesies, earth changes, probable futures, and their effect on seeking truth. You will notice that we didn't linger long here this time.

I think it is important, in the context of this little volume of fragments we kept out of the first four volumes of The Law of One, *that we look straight and hard at the tendency of UFO researchers and people in general to see conspiracies and treachery behind every bush and gossip item. When I first started reading in this area, in the late sixties, there were prophets claiming a near future in which war, catastrophe, and desolation would reign. In the years since, nothing has changed but the dates. Always this great trouble is seen to be coming a couple of years from now, and the call is to put all else aside except for preparing for this time of trial. I have known people of sound judgment who have basement walls lined with freeze-dried food, proof against disaster. Let's call it the bomb shelter syndrome.*

The thing I wish to emphasize is that these thoughts do harm to the innocent future. They take present energy away from the immediate happenings of the day, and sap it with chronic fear and fear-based planning. Disasters do occur, indubitably. And when they do come, we can hope simply to meet them with some grace. In that day, it will be the people who have learned to live from a loving heart that will be able to help the most, not the people who have barricaded themselves into a mindset based on fear.

Session 65, August 8, 1981

QUESTIONER: Are you saying then that this possible condition of war would be much more greatly spread across the surface of the globe than anything we have experienced in the past, and therefore touch a larger percentage of the population in this form of catalyst?

RA: I am Ra. This is correct. There are those now experimenting with one of the major weapons of this scenario; that is, the so-called psychotronic group of devices which are being experimentally used to cause such alterations in wind and weather as will result in eventual famine. If this program is not countered and proves experimentally satisfactory, the methods in this scenario would be made public. There would then be what those whom you call Russians hope to be a bloodless invasion of their personnel in this and every land deemed valuable. However, the peoples of your culture have little propensity for bloodless surrender.

Fragment 37

There were no great tricks or elaborate rituals employed to aid Carla in maintaining her physical health and her ability to serve as the instrument for this contact. Good foods, reasonable exercise, and a healthy and happy attitude are techniques that are within most people's reach.

It was not very much fun to be so scrutinized for estimation of my energy level in this way. I have always had tons of mental, emotional, and spiritual energy, but low physical energy. In fact I would say my life has been lived mainly on nerve. To me, life has always seemed a marvelous celebration, a party of sun and moon and earth and sky, birdsong and green leaves, and people of every sort and kind, doing various amazing things. This joy in life is a pure gift, and it has made my life a dream of love. It was no surprise to me when Ra spoke of my low energy! And I doubt any athlete worked harder to keep in shape than I did during this time.

Session 66,
August 12, 1981

QUESTIONER: Would you give me an indication of the instrument's condition?

RA: I am Ra. The vital energies are somewhat depleted at this time, but not seriously so. The physical energy level is extremely low. Otherwise, it is as previously stated.

QUESTIONER: Is there anything that we can do, staying within the first distortion, to seek aid from the Confederation in order to alleviate the instrument's physical problems?

RA: I am Ra. No.

QUESTIONER: Can you tell me the most appropriate method in attempting to alleviate the instrument's physical problems?

RA: I am Ra. The basic material has been covered before concerning the nurturing of this instrument. We recapitulate: the exercise according to ability, not to exceed appropriate parameters, the nutrition, the social intercourse with companions, the sexual activity in green ray or above, and in general, the sharing of the distortions of this group's individual experiences in an helpful, loving manner.
These things are being accomplished with what we consider great harmony, given the density in which you dance. The specific attention and activities, with which those with physical complex distortions may alleviate these distortions, are known to this instrument.
Finally, it is well for this instrument to continue the practices it has lately begun.

QUESTIONER: Which practices are those?

RA: I am Ra. These practices concern exercises which we have outlined previously. We may say that the variety of experiences which this entity seeks is helpful, as we have said before, but as this instrument works in these practices the distortion seems less mandatory.

Fragment 38

In the first question, Don is asking Ra how we could resolve the seeming paradox of being able to serve various portions of the same Creator, some of which rejoiced at our service and some of which wished nothing less than to remove the instrument and the contact from the third density (i.e., our fifth-density, negative friend). We removed the sentence that you see in brackets because we did not wish for overattention to be given to our personalities. We include it now because it might be helpful for those who have the feeling that they may be here from elsewhere to know that there is a kind of momentum of serving others that adds its support to the individual's desire to learn and to serve well.

Those who have read *The Crucifixion of Esmerelda Sweetwater* will recognize the last query of this section. This book was written by Don and Carla in 1968, when they first got together and formed L/L Research. It was their first project and was unusual in that it seemed to be seen first and then recorded as a story. And it was also unusual in the fact that it seemed to anticipate many of the experiences that Don and Carla, and later I, would share in their work together.

Into this first work of ours was poured all the love we had for each other and for the ideals and concerns of a purer, higher way, a way of love undefiled by any hint of the heaviness of earth. We were smitten with each other; it was a wonderful time. Mind you, Don was never verbal, but this time held our short-lived intimate physical relationship, which I treasure, and our time of that nearly trembling joy one has when one is in love. The story seemed to tell itself, and we saw the characters so clearly they might have been telling us the story over our shoulder. The only part of the book that was in error was the ending. The character that rather resembled me on a perfect day was killed off by the bad guys at the end of the book. In real life, my frail body was stronger than Don's, due, I think, to my gifts of faith and élan vital. Don was never the least bit at home on this earth. He lived his life very defended and isolated, except for me and a very few close friends and relations. One thing is sure: his gifts have been well shared in the body of work that comprises the material Ra shared with us. His questions were marvels of sense and always game to head in a new direction. The romance ended badly, in the sense that Don has entered a larger life, and I have been left to become a whole different person than the one he groomed and appreciated. But the work has not ended at all and will not until the world no longer has any need of our material.

Session 67,
August 15, 1981

QUESTIONER: Then how could we solve this paradox? [The sentence of personal material that was removed from Ra's answer is inserted in this paragraph, which may be found on p. 122 of Book III.]

RA: I am Ra. Consider, if you will, that you have no ability not to serve the Creator, since all is the Creator. In your individual growth patterns appear the basic third-density choice. [Further, there are overlaid memories of the positive polarizations of your home density.] Thus, your particular orientation is strongly polarized towards service to others and has attained wisdom as well as compassion.

QUESTIONER: Are you familiar with a book that the instrument and I wrote approximately twelve years ago, called *The Crucifixion of Esmerelda Sweetwater*, in particular the banishing ritual that we used to bring the entities to Earth?

RA: I am Ra. This is correct.

QUESTIONER: Were there any incorrectnesses in our writing with respect to the way this was performed?

RA: I am Ra. The incorrectnesses occurred only due to the difficulty an author would have in describing the length of training necessary to enable the ones known in that particular writing as Theodore and Pablo in the necessary disciplines.

QUESTIONER: It has seemed to me that that book has somehow, in its entirety, been a link to many of those whom we have met since we wrote it, and to many of the activities we have experienced. Is this correct?

RA: I am Ra. This is quite so.

Fragment 39
In seeking advice from Ra on caring for Carla's condition and in scheduling sessions, we again found that Ra constantly guarded our free will by providing loosely formed guidelines that offered us direction but required that we continually exercise our ability and duty to make the decisions ourselves. Thus was the contact a function of our free will by

the fact that information was given only in response to questions, that the kind of information was determined by the nature of our seeking being formed into such and such a question, and by the actual scheduling or timing of sessions. So it is necessary for each seeker of truth to decide what to seek, how to seek, and when to seek. Not everyone speaks so directly to Ra, but everyone speaks with the One Creator in one form or another. If the seeking is strong enough, any portion of the Creator can teach you all that you wish to know. It is the seeking that determines the finding.

The last two questions and answers refer to a most unusual phenomenon that we discovered was a possibility in Session 68; that is, the misplacement of the mind/body/spirit complex of the instrument, under certain unprotected conditions, by the fifth-density, negative entity that monitored our Ra sessions. This possibility was unusual enough, but to add to its extraordinary nature is the fact that Don and Carla wrote about an identical situation in *The Crucifixion of Esmerelda Sweetwater* thirteen years earlier. The ending of the book was not seen as was the remainder of the book, and it had to be written in the usual way. Now this all makes sense to us, for it seems that the ending of that book was a symbolic description of Don's death in November 1984.

Have you ever been put on the spot by someone asking how you were? Usually, the civil greeting "How are you?" is a meaningless murmur indicating respect and awareness of presence, rather than a true request for information. The last thing wanted is a laundry list of woes and ailments. So I was not accustomed to being so in touch with myself that I could tell my exact condition. When one is in pain all the time, as I have been for a long time now, the stimulus eventually becomes dulled and ignored simply because it is telling one nothing useful. When one has done all one can, one is far better off simply getting on with the life that is offered. This may sound extreme, but I know just how many chronic-pain patients there are out there, quietly dealing with life, usually very well indeed. So the last thing I would wish is to be constantly checking to see my energy level. My reaction, at that time and at this one, is "Ya gotta be kidding!" I cannot remember ever having physical energy. Mental, emotional, spiritual energy, oh YES! Tons of that I have, and a heart full of joy to be here, whatever my limitations. But I run on nerve alone, in my own perception. So this concern, while genuine and necessary, was a challenge to me. I really wanted to do sessions so much, also, which biased my response.

The matter of The Crucifixion of Esmerelda Sweetwater *playing itself out in real life is to me a fascinating example of the liquidity and permeability of the supposed boundaries of space and time. We saw that story as if it were a movie running in our heads. We wrote it never knowing it had* to do with us in the future. It was most unsettling when the more tragic parts of the book played themselves out with horrid accuracy. Life humbles one again and again, bringing us all to our knees and revealing self to self in utter fidelity. As always when I think on Don's death, I am warmed by the perfection of his opening to love and his nobility, as I am chilled by his absence from my side. One can do little except offer it all up to the Creator in thanksgiving and praise.

Session 68,
August 18, 1981

QUESTIONER: Could you first please give me an indication of the instrument's condition?

RA: I am Ra. This instrument's physical energies are depleted completely. The remainder is as previously stated.

QUESTIONER: With the physical energies completely depleted, should I continue with the session? I'm not sure exactly what that means.

RA: I am Ra. We have available transferred energy which is due to the service offered by two of this group, and, therefore we are able to continue. Were it not for this transferred energy, the instrument, whose will is strong, would have depleted its vital energies by willing the available resources. Thus if there is no transfer of energy, and if the instrument seems depleted to the extent it now is, it is well to refrain from using the instrument. If there is energy transferred, this service may be accepted without damage to the distortion of normal vital energy.

We may note that the physical energy has been exhausted, not due to the distortion toward pain, although this is great at this space/time, but primarily due to the cumulative effects of continual experience of this distortion.

QUESTIONER: Would you recommend a greater rest period between the end of this work period and the next work period? Would that help the instrument?

RA: I am Ra. We might suggest, as always, that the support group watch the instrument with care and make the decision based upon observation. It is not within our capacity to specifically recommend a future decision. We would note that our previous recommendation of one working on alternate diurnal periods did not take into account the fragility of the instrument, and thus we would ask your forgiveness for this suggestion.

At this nexus, our distortion is towards a flexible scheduling of workings based upon, as we said, the support group's decisions concerning the instrument. We would again note that there is a fine line between the care of the instrument for continued use which we find acceptable and the proper understanding, if you will excuse this misnomer, of the entire group's need to work in service.

Thus, if the instrument's condition is truly marginal, by all means let more rest occur between workings. However, if there is desire for the working and the instrument is at all able in your careful opinion, it is, shall we say, a well-done action for this group to work. We cannot be more precise, for this contact is a function of your free will.

QUESTIONER: We have been speaking almost precisely of a portion of the Esmerelda Sweetwater book which we wrote, having to do with the character Trostrick's misplacement of the space girl's mind/body/spirit complex. What is the significance of that work which we did with respect to our lives? It has been confusing to me for some time as to how it meshes in. Can you tell me that?

RA: I am Ra. We scan each and find we may speak.

QUESTIONER: Would you please do so now?

RA: I am Ra. We confirm the following, which is already, shall we say, supposed or hypothesized.

When the commitment was made between two of this group to work for the betterment of the planetary sphere, this commitment activated a possibility/probability vortex of some strength. The experience of generating this volume was unusual in that it was visualized as if watching the moving picture.

Time had become available in its present-moment form. The scenario of the volume went smoothly until the ending of the volume. You could not end the volume, and the ending was not visualized as the entire body of the material but was written or authored.

This is due to the action of free will in all of the creation. However, the volume contains a view of significant events, both symbolically and specifically, which you saw under the influence of the magnetic attraction which was released when the commitment was made and full memory of the dedication of this, what you may call, mission restored.

Fragment 40

The time/space or metaphysical portion of ourselves is not apparent to any of us most of the time, yet it is the place or realm of our truer being. This is true for anyone. It is the essence from which that which we know of as our conscious selves manifests as a portion of our true selves. Our space/time, physical selves are a reflection or shadow of our true selves, which those who have eyes that can see behind illusion see when they behold our time/space beingness. It was this metaphysical self that Ra observed when first considering our group as a potential group for contact.

Don, Jim, and I had a common interest in spiritual community before we ever got together. When we did join households at Christmas in 1980, we consciously joined together as a light group. We wanted to live a spiritually directed life with each other and serve as we might. Much was sacrificed for this joining, on both Jim's and Don's parts, for they were both loners, fond of their own company and not much fond of society, although they were both excellent hosts when guests did come by. But the sacrifices were gladly made, and we felt very blessed to be together. When the Ra contact began three weeks later, we felt very happy that we had gone ahead on faith and joined forces.

What we had together was that clear, pure, unmuddied love and fellowship that stems from there being no fear between us, or needs that were not met. For a golden few months and years, this remained so. I have long felt that Don's decline and death were the result of his becoming fearful that I might leave him for Jim. I would never have done such a thing and had no idea he was concerned. But I believe that this fear, which he never expressed, and which I knew nothing of, led to his woeful last months, in which he suffered so greatly.

Session 71,
September 18, 1981

QUESTIONER: When you say you searched for this group, what do you mean? What was your process of search? I ask this question to understand more the illusion of time and space.

RA: I am Ra. Consider the process of one who sees the spectrograph of some complex of elements. It is a complex paint sample, let us say, for ease of description. We of Ra knew the needed elements for communication which had any chance of enduring. We compared our color chip to many individuals and groups over a long span of your time. Your spectrograph matches our sample.

The Law of One

In response to your desire to see the relationship betwixt space/time and time/space, may we say that we conducted this search in time/space, for in this illusion, one may quite readily see entities as vibratory complexes and groups as harmonics within vibratory complexes.

Fragment 41

In Session 75 we were trying to help Carla through her upcoming hand operation in a local hospital. When the Ra contact began, the pre-incarnatively chosen arthritic limitations set in more strongly than ever, and Carla's desire to do things for others with hands that were meant to be restricted from mundane work brought more and more pain and damage to the arthritic joints—thus necessitating the operation for short-term repair. The length or success of the surgical repairs would depend upon Carla's growing ability to accept the limitations that she placed upon herself before the incarnation, in order that her focus might move inward and prepare her for the possibility of becoming a channel. Her ability to accept these limitations delayed the next surgery for four years.

Since she had been a Christian mystic from birth, certain prayers of her Episcopalian church, and the communion service in particular, were felt by Ra to be of aid to her. The Banishing Ritual of the Lesser Pentagram, which we had been using for some time to purify our place of working for the Ra contact, was suggested for her hospital room and the operating room. The greatest protective and healing device, however, was seen to be love, whether manifest or unspoken, for all any ritual such as prayer, communion, or the Banishing Ritual of the Lesser Pentagram actually does is alert positively polarized, discarnate entities so that they may provide that quality that we call love from their quarters, for whatever the purpose might be. Each of us may also provide that same love as a function of our truly caring for another. As we learn the lessons of love within this third-density illusion, we are also learning the basics of healing and protection.

There are surprises in this material, even after all these years. It was not until this moment (writing in 1997) that Jim and I realized we did not follow one of Ra's suggestions during that hospital experience. Jim, Don, and I vibrated the Banishing Ritual twice a day; Jim and I both remember that. Neither of us can recall reading the Mass in any form. We just missed it. Imagine wasting Ra's advice! I know we did not do that on purpose. After sixteen years, all we can say is that refrain of bozos everywhere . . . oops!

As to the hand-holding when I meditated, this was a practice that began after a particularly discomfiting experience during one of our public meditation sessions. These were completely separate from the sessions with Ra. Any and all could come and check us out. I did not go into trance at these sessions as I did with Ra sessions, but channeled from a very light trance state. However, during the question-and-answer period, someone asked a question that I had no earthly idea about, and I thought to myself, "I wish I were channeling Ra." Immediately I began to leave my body, which was absolutely NOT to be done, according to Ra. The source that I was channeling, Latwii, simply kept me channeling—probably pure nonsense—but it sufficed to keep me in the body. After that, someone, usually Jim, always held my hand during sessions. To this day, Jim holds my hand as we meditate during our morning offering, and at all meditation sessions we offer. Better safe than sorry is the cliché that covers this.

I remember with great affection the utter fidelity of love and concern that Don and Jim showed me during this time. It was very hard for Don especially to see me in pain. But he did not flinch or draw away but rather tried ceaselessly to protect and aid me. The same could be said of Jim, but I think it was light-years harder for Don to bear this than Jim. Jim is a simple, straightforward person. To him, what is, is. I remember asking him once if all he was going to say in this life was "yup, nope, or maybe." "Yup," he replied. Then, after considering, he said, "Nope . . ." Then more consideration, and he finally settled on, "Maybe!" To Don my pain was his pain, for we were truly one being in that ineffable sense that is beyond space and time. The pain, severe though it was, did not overly distress me, but it foundered Don. His level of concern was profound.

Through the years since this channeling, I have more and more come to appreciate Ra's suggestion that I fully accept my limitations. After my miraculous rehabilitation in 1992, I found myself out of the wheelchair and vertical for the first time in many years. A year ago, I was able to give the downstairs hospital bed back to Medicare (I still find one helpful at night, for sleeping). When I first started to rebuild a "vertical" life, I was full of ideas as to what I might accomplish. I tried going back to school to get myself current in my old field of library service. I tried to take a job. I volunteered at church, far beyond my actual capacity to serve. And this took its toll, as I collected injuries, a broken ankle, sprained knees, and two more hand operations. Finally, about a year ago, I managed to pare down my work to the point where I allowed much rest time within the schedule of the day. I've tinkered with this schedule, finding ways to harmonize my efforts with Jim's, finding how to nurture myself, finding what priorities my life really has. I am hopeful that I have at this point realized these set limits to effort, and have begun to cooperate with my destiny.

I fully respect my pre-incarnative choice to take on these uncomfortable limitations. The experience has hollowed me out and made me an ever better channel. I continue to rejoice as I see little bits of my ego fall away. My prayer these days is "Lord, show me Thy ways." There is much work left for me, a true idiot. But I exult in being upon the King's Highway.

Session 75,
October 31, 1981

QUESTIONER: Could you first please give me the condition of the instrument?

RA: I am Ra. It is as previously stated, with some slight lessening of the reserve of vital energy due to mental/emotional distortions regarding what you call the future.

QUESTIONER: I felt that this session was advisable before the instrument has her hospital experience. She wished to ask a few questions, if possible, about that.

First, is there anything that the instrument or we might do to improve the hospital experience or to aid the instrument in any way with respect to this?

RA: I am Ra. Yes. There are ways of aiding the mental/emotional state of this entity, with the notation that this is so only for this entity or one of like distortions. There is also a general thing which may be accomplished to improve the location which is called the hospital.

The first aiding has to do with the vibration of the ritual with which this entity is most familiar, and which this entity has long used to distort its perception of the One Infinite Creator. This is an helpful thing at any point in the diurnal period but is especially helpful as your sun body removes itself from your local sight.

The general improvement of the place where the performance of the ritual of the purification is to be performed is known. We may note that the distortion towards love, as you call this spiritual/emotional complex which is felt by each for this entity, will be of aid whether this is expressed or unmanifest, as there is no protection greater than love.

QUESTIONER: Do you mean that it would be valuable to perform the Banishing Ritual of the Lesser Pentagram in the room in which she will be occupying in the hospital?

RA: I am Ra. This is correct.

QUESTIONER: I was wondering about the operating room. That might be very difficult. Would it be helpful there?

RA: I am Ra. This is correct. We may note that it is always helpful. Therefore, it is not easy to posit a query to which you would not receive the answer which we offer. This does not indicate that it is essential to purify a place. The power of visualization may aid in your support where you cannot intrude in your physical form.

QUESTIONER: I see the way to do this as a visualization of the operating room and a visualization of the three of us performing the banishing ritual in the room as we perform it at another location. Is this the correct procedure?

RA: I am Ra. This is one correct method of achieving your desired configuration.

QUESTIONER: Is there a better method than that?

RA: I am Ra. There are better methods for those more practiced. For this group, this method is well.

QUESTIONER: I would assume those more practiced would leave their physical bodies and, in the other body, enter the room and practice the ritual. Is this what you mean?

RA: I am Ra. This is correct.

QUESTIONER: The instrument would like to know if she can meditate in the hospital without someone holding her hand. Would this be a safe practice?

RA: I am Ra. We might suggest that the instrument may pray with safety but only meditate with another entity's tactile protection.

QUESTIONER: The instrument would like to know what she can do to improve the condition of her back, as she feels it will be a problem for the operation.

RA: I am Ra. As we scan the physical complex, we find several factors contributing to one general distortion experienced by the instrument. Two of these distortions have been diagnosed; one has not; nor will the entity be willing to accept the chemicals sufficient to cause cessation of this distortion you call pain.

In general we may say that the sole modality addressing itself specifically to all three contributing distortions, which is not now being used, is that of the warmed water, which is moved with gentle force repeatedly against the entire physical complex while the physical vehicle is seated. This would be of some aid if practiced daily after the exercise period.

QUESTIONER: Did the exercise of the fire performed before the session help the instrument?

RA: I am Ra. There was some slight physical aid to the instrument. This will enlarge itself as the practitioner learns/teaches its healing art. Further, there is distortion in the mental/emotional complex which feeds the vital energy towards comfort, due to support which tends to build up the level of vital energy, as this entity is a sensitive instrument.

QUESTIONER: Was the exercise of the fire properly done?

RA: I am Ra. The baton is well visualized. The conductor will learn to hear the entire score of the great music of its art.

QUESTIONER: I assume that if this can be fully accomplished, that exercise will result in total healing of the distortions of the instrument to such an extent that operations would be unnecessary. Is this correct?

RA: I am Ra. No.

QUESTIONER: What else is necessary, the instrument's acceptance?

RA: I am Ra. This is correct. The case with this instrument being delicate, since it must totally accept much which the limitations it now experiences cause to occur involuntarily. This is a pre-incarnative choice.

Fragment 42

Ra mentioned a number of times that impatience is one of the most frequent catalysts with which the seeker must work. When a general outline of the path of evolution is seen, it is often too enticing to resist jumping ahead of one's actual place upon the path and making quickly for the goal. This was the case for me as I queried about the steps of accepting the self that I had discovered in my own seeking. Ra's suggestion to carefully place the foundation of one's house before hanging the roof seems sound. It brings to mind the old saying "There is never time enough to do a thing right the first time, but there is always time enough to do it over."

Note also how any thought and action, when carefully scrutinized, can lead one to the basic distortions or lessons that one is working on. Thus, any portion of the life experience can be seen as a holographic miniature of the entire incarnational plan for an entity, as layer upon layer of meaning is discovered behind the smallest surface of things. As we discovered in Book IV, this is not because the events in our world are naturally filled with layers of meanings—though this is also true—but because we subconsciously color the events in our lives in the way that we have pre-incarnatively decided will provide us with the opportunities to learn what we wish to learn. That's why different people see the same catalyst in different ways—often wildly varying. As we work with these colorations/distortions/reactions in a conscious manner, we begin to accept ourselves for having them because we begin to see the purpose behind them. This acceptance draws to us the balancing attitudes for our distortion, so that our viewpoint expands and we are able to accept and love another part of the Creator that was previously not accepted and loved. Love, then, is the potential product of any distortion.

The course of spiritual seeking is often unclear, and seekers are always looking hopefully for some single point of clarity to hold against the universe as yardstick. Certainly, the remembrance of Love Itself suffices in this wise. But this remembrance comes slowly when we are caught up in our reactions. We each have these hooks that catch us up, and there is some time that passes before we are reoriented. We wish we were more alert! But we are not always attentive, no matter how abreast of things we hope to be. I like Ra's insistence that we continue to catch ourselves in the act, rather than swinging around in a supposed shortcut that keeps us from seeing into why we got caught. It is a real breakthrough for me every time I see myself GETTING caught. This moment reveals to us that inner distortion we've been looking for! Once we can see the mechanism, we can far more effectually work on its release. I think the goal here is not to be without error, but to see our errors more clearly. We are human: we will err. It is impossible not to. But we can, slowly, learn ourselves well enough to do the erring during inner processes, rather than upon the outer world stage. Perhaps, one day, all the "buttons" from childhood and other traumas might become released, and we be clear. And perhaps not. I don't think this matters nearly as much as how much we have loved.

Session 82,
March 27, 1982

QUESTIONER: Jim has a personal question that is not to be published. He asks, "It seems that my balancing work has shifted from more-peripheral concerns such as patience/impatience, to learning to open myself in unconditional love, to accepting my self as whole and perfect, and then to accepting my self as the Creator. If this is a normal progression of focus for balancing, wouldn't it be more efficient once this is discovered for a person to work on the acceptance of the self as Creator rather than work peripherally on the secondary and tertiary results of not accepting the self?"

RA: I am Ra. The term "efficiency" has misleading connotations. In the context of doing work in the disciplines of the personality, in order to be of more full efficiency in the central acceptance of the self, it is first quite necessary to know the distortions of the self which the entity is accepting. Each thought and action needs must then be scrutinized for the precise foundation of the distortions of any reactions. This process shall lead to the more central task of acceptance. However, the architrave must be in place before the structure is built.

Fragment 43

The first portion of Session 84 is mostly nuts-and-bolts maintenance of the instrument. Her primary exercise each day was one hour of brisk walking, and when her feet began to suffer injury, we tried alternating two different kinds of shoes, hoping that each would aid one portion of the injury without aggravating another portion.

Don also asked Ra about information concerning earth changes, which Andrija Puharich had received from one of his sources. Instead of responding directly to the query and risking infringing upon the free will of Dr. Puharich, Ra chose to speak to the subject of earth changes as representative of one of two choices that a person may make in the search for truth.

Between that response and the last question and answer that you see was a portion of information concerning a person's encounter with a UFO, which Ra asked us to keep private. The question and answer that you do see is in reference to this same

UFO contact and reveals the general way in which many face-to-face encounters between our third-density population and extraterrestrial entities occur. What is actually remembered by the third-density entity is a product of its expectations and what its subconscious mind fashions as an acceptable story that will allow the entity to continue functioning without losing its mental balance. This is the nature of the positive contact in which the third-density entity is being awakened to seek more clearly the nature of not only the UFO encounter but the life pattern as well. Negative contacts, however, utilize the concepts of fear and doom to further separate and confuse the Earth population.

My poor feet! Rheumatoid disease is notorious for its depredations upon one's extremities, and perhaps my hands, feet, and neck have suffered the worst from its progression. Thirteen operations on my hands and six on my feet have staved off total dysfunction, but the old digits are not what they once were. During these sessions, they suffered far more than normal, because when I was in trance, I did not move at all. Those of Ra did not know how to make my body move very well, and so whatever aches and pains I had became rapidly very hard to bear. It was easy for me to be discouraged. I can remember asking the Creator, with some asperity, what It had in mind when it gave me these gifts! How inconvenient! Especially in terms of this contact, which we all knew was special, I tended to feel that I had let down the side by these sore joints taking time away from the sessions in length. Feeling unworthy in the first place, I felt sheepish that I was, by these distortions, lessening the content of each working. At this latter day, however, I have ceased to rail against whatever comes my way. I am just glad to be here. And if I can still channel, fine. But I think all of us have one main job, and that is just to be who we are, living in an open-hearted love of the Creator and His creation.

Ra's zinger of an answer to Puharich's question about coming earth changes is worth pondering in depth. The answer concerning the person's remembrance of a close encounter of the third kind, being on board a craft, is also pithy. We really have a great deal to do with how we experience events of an archetypal nature, and this bleeds through into the everyday. So much of what we receive from the world is set by what we give to it. Ra's comments are provocative in suggesting how we can view that ineffable thing called sanity.

Session 84,
April 14, 1982

QUESTIONER: What disease in particular were you speaking of and what would be its cause?

RA: I am Ra. One disease, as you call this distortion, is that of the arthritis and the lupus erythematosus. The cause of this complex of distortions is, at base, pre-incarnative. We refrain from determining the other distortion potential at this space/time due to our desire to maintain the free will of this group. Affirmations may yet cause this difficulty to resolve itself. Therefore, we simply encourage the general care with the diet with the instructions about allergy, as you call this quite complex distortion of the mind and body complexes.

QUESTIONER: Could you make any suggestions about the instrument's feet or how they got in the bad shape that they are in, and if alternating the shoes would help?

RA: I am Ra. The distortion referred to above—that is, the complex of juvenile rheumatoid arthritis and lupus erythematosus—acts in such a way as to cause various portions of the body complex to become distorted in the way in which the instrument's pedal appendages are now distorted.

We may suggest care in resumption of the exercise, but determination as well. The alternation of footwear shall prove efficacious. The undergarment for the feet, which you call the anklet, should be of a softer and finer material than is now being used, and should, if possible, conform more to the outline of those appendages upon which it is placed. This should provide a more efficient aid to the cushioning of these appendages.

We may further suggest that the same immersion in the waters which is helpful to the general distortion is, in general, helpful to this specific distortion as well. However, the injury which has been sustained in the metatarsal region of the right pedal appendage should be further treated for some period of your space/time by the prudent application of the ice to the arch of the right foot for brief periods, followed always by immersion in the warm water.

QUESTIONER: I am sure that we are getting into a problem area with the first distortion here, with a difficulty with a bit of transient material, but I have questions from a couple of people that I would like to ask. The first one especially is of no lasting value. Andrija Puharich asks about the coming physical changes, specifically this summer. Is there anything that we could relay to him about that?

RA: I am Ra. We may confirm the good intention of the source of this entity's puzzles and suggest that it is a grand choice that each may make to, by desire, collect the details of the day or, by desire, seek the keys to unknowing.

QUESTIONER: I can't help but be interested in the fact that this other entity to whom we were previously referring reported being taken on board a craft. Could you tell me something about that?

RA: I am Ra. The nature of contact is such that in order for the deep portion of the trunk of the tree of mind affected to be able to accept the contact, some symbology which may rise to the conscious mind is necessary as a framework for the explanation of the fruits of the contact. In such cases the entity's own expectations fashion the tale which shall be most acceptable to that entity, and in the dream state, or a trance state in which visions may be produced, this seeming memory is fed into the higher levels of the so-called subconscious and the lower levels of the conscious. From this point the story may surface as any memory and cause the instrument to function without losing balance or sanity.

Fragment 44
The gift of a crystal that has been charged by a friend is a very special gift. Apparently, it is also the kind of gift that creates a special connection between the one who gives it and the one who receives it, and because of this connection it would seem that a special care needs to be exercised both by the one who would give and the one who would receive such a crystal as a gift.

People like myself, who are sensitive to energy flow, often find that they simply cannot ignore certain crystals. I do not wear them at all, having found that their energy can disturb me, make me edgy. In these latter days of crystal technology, it is not surprising that crystals can be seen to have power. It is their magnetization by the people who have them, or give them, that makes them unique beyond their structure's singularity. They need to be handled with care, I think. I have been told many stories of the effects, good and bad, of such magnetized stones.

If you receive one or are drawn to one, be sure to cleanse it in salt water overnight, and then magnetize it for your own use by holding it during meditation and asking silently that it be blessed for service.

Session 88,
May 29, 1982

QUESTIONER: Is the small crystal that the instrument uses upon her during the session of any benefit or detriment?

RA: I am Ra. This crystal is beneficial as long as he who has charged it is functioning in a positively oriented manner.

QUESTIONER: Who charged the crystal?

RA: I am Ra. This crystal was charged for use by this instrument by the one known as Neil.

QUESTIONER: It would be an abridgment of the first distortion for you to tell us if he is still functioning in a positive manner, would it not?

RA: I am Ra. We perceive you have replied to your own query.

Fragment 45

The first few questions and responses in this session are more of the nuts-and-bolts maintenance that we constantly found ourselves having to deal with in keeping up both with Carla's arthritic flare-ups of pain and our fifth-density, negative friend's accentuating of these difficulties.

Toward the beginning of Session 92 in Book IV of *The Law of One*, one of Ra's responses was "There is the need for the instrument to choose the manner of its beingness. It has the distortion, as we have noted, towards the martyrdom. This can be evaluated and choices made only by the entity." And at the end of that same session, Ra added, "The instrument, itself, might ponder some earlier words and consider their implications. We say this because the continued calling upon vital energies, if allowed to proceed to the end of the vital energy, will end this contact. There is not the need for continued calling upon these energies. The instrument must find the key to this riddle or face a growing loss of this particular service at this particular space/time nexus." The last part of the personal material from Session 94 consists of a query from Carla upon which she pondered long, concerning the riddle that Ra had presented in Session 92. The riddle was Ra's way of maintaining Carla's free will and at the same time giving her a direction for thought that might enhance both her own growth and the service of the contact to others.

As time went on, we fiddled around more and more with clothing and such, trying to maximize my comfort and the length of sessions. I was warmly clothed, all in white, with the white comforter placed so it did not drag down the arms, and then my hands were gloved, and the kind of tubing used to vent washer/dryers went over both hands up to about the elbow, to keep the weight of the cover off them completely. It was a job just getting dressed for the sessions. It seems almost funny when one looks back on it, that we kept on with such perseverance. But at the time, there was only one thought among us three, and that was to continue this contact and learn all we could. I think if it happened again, I'd do the same thing again: give my utmost. And I imagine Jim would say the same. Without question, Don was also absolutely single-minded about pursuing the questioning with Ra. He felt that this was the culmination of his life's work. If we were somewhat wearied and even battered by the conditions we had to work in, that was acceptable. And we did indeed all feel the weariness.

I appreciate the point those of Ra make concerning my gift of faith. It has been true for as long as I can remember that I have enjoyed that attitude of faith and hope. It may well be why I am alive today, while Don is a soldier fallen in the spiritual battle. Don was a person of infinite dignity, intelligence, and ethical purity, but always a somewhat melancholy man under the mask of polite courtesy, efficiency, and professorial charm that he wore to meet the world. Much has been given me in this life in the way of gifts, but this is surely the most precious.

Doesn't Ra offer a marvelous perspective to the myopic spiritual eye, in suggesting that I was only looking at what still needed doing, rather than giving thanks for what had come around already? I have often taken their advice and pondered the merits of judging as the stern critic that would have everything just so. Life is messy, and often things are very much untidy, and that needs to be released, forgiven, and accepted.

And Ra's final thought is truly a jewel. What, after all, is all our striving in the end, including this contact and all human thought, but a vain and empty folly? We cannot move from illusion to truth in this body, on this plane of existence. So where is our truest and central service? Not in the doing but in the being, in allowing the true self, that open-hearted lover of all things in creation, to share its essence with the world, and to allow the love and light of the Infinite One to pass through it and radiate into the planetary consciousness. That is our true geste, all of us who have come here at this time to be of service: being, living a devotional and devoted life.

Session 94,
August 26, 1982

QUESTIONER: I have questions here from the instrument. The first one is "Is our fifth-density friend responsible for the instrument's extreme distortion towards pain during and just after sessions?"

RA: I am Ra. Yes.

QUESTIONER: Is there anything that we can do that we are not doing to remedy this situation, so that the instrument does not experience this pain, or as much pain?

RA: I am Ra. There is little that can be done due to a complex of preexisting distortions. The distortions are triple in the source.

There is the, shall we say, less than adequate work of your chirurgeons which allows for various distortions in the left wrist area.

There is the distortion called systemic lupus erythematosus which causes the musculature of the lower left and right arms to allow for distortions in the normal, shall we say, configuration of both.

Lastly, there is the nerve damage, more especially to the left, but in both appendages from the thoracic outlet.

In the course of the waking behavior, the instrument can respond to the various signals which ring the tocsin of pain, thus alerting the mind complex, which in turn moves the physical complex in many and subtle configurations which relieve the various distortions. Your friend greets these distortions, as has been stated before, immediately prior to the beginning of the working. However, during the working the instrument is not with its yellow-ray chemical vehicle, and thusly the many small movements which could most effectively aid in the decrease of these distortions are not possible. Ra must carefully examine the mental configurations of the mind complex in order to make even the grossest manipulation. It is not our skill to use a yellow-ray vehicle.

The weight of the cover has some deleterious effect upon these distortions in some cases, and thus we mentioned that there was a small thing which could be done; that is, the framing of that which lifted the coverlet from the body slightly. In order to compensate for loss of warmth, the wearing of material warming the manual appendages would then be indicated.

QUESTIONER: I immediately think of the instrument wearing long underwear under the robe that it now wears, and an extremely light, white cover. Would this be satisfactory?

RA: I am Ra. Due to this instrument's lack of radiant physical energy, the heavier cover is suggested.

QUESTIONER: In your statement, at the beginning of it, you said "less than adequate work of" and then there was a word that I didn't understand at all. Are you familiar with the word that I am trying to understand?

RA: I am Ra. No.

QUESTIONER: Then we'll have to wait until we transcribe the material. I assume that our fifth-density, negative friend doesn't cause these distortions all of the time, because he wishes to emphasize the fact that the instrument is going to be distorted only if she attempts one of these service-to-others workings and, therefore, attempts to stifle the workings. Is this correct?

RA: I am Ra. This is partially correct. The incorrect portion is this: The entity of which you speak has found its puissance[1] less than adequate to mount a continuous assault upon this instrument's physical vehicle and has, shall we say, chosen the more effective of the space/time nexi of this instrument's experience for its service.

QUESTIONER: Could you tell me why I have felt so tired on several recent occasions?

RA: I am Ra. This has been covered in previous material.
The contact which you now experience costs a certain amount of the energy which each of the group brought into manifestation in the present incarnation. Although the brunt of this cost falls upon the instrument, it is caparisoned by pre-incarnative design with the light and gladsome armor of faith and will to a far more conscious extent than most mind/body/spirit complexes are able to enjoy without much training and initiation.
Those of the support group also offer the essence of will and faith in service to others, supporting the instrument as it releases itself completely in the service of the One Creator. Therefore, each of the support group also experiences a weariness of the spirit which is indistinguishable from physical-energy deficit, except that if each experiments with this weariness, each shall discover the physical energy in its usual distortion.

QUESTIONER: Thank you. I didn't mean to go over previous material. I should have phrased my question more carefully. That is what I expected. I was trying to get a confirmation of my suspicion. I suspected that. I will try to be more careful in questioning.
The second question from the instrument says, "While on vacation I uncovered a lot about myself not consciously known before. It seems to me that I have coasted a lot on the spiritual gifts given at birth, and never have spent any time getting to know my human self which seems to be a child, immature and irrational. Is this so?"

RA: I am Ra. This is partially correct.

QUESTIONER: Then she says, "If this is so, this seems to be part of the riddle about the manner of my beingness that Ra spoke of. I fear that if I do not work successfully on my human distortions, I shall be responsible for losing the contact. Yet, also Ra suggests the over-dedication to any outcome is unwise. Could Ra comment on these thoughts?"

RA: I am Ra. We comment in general first upon the query about the contact which indicates once again that the instrument views the mind/body/spirit complex with jaundiced eye. Each mind/body/spirit complex that is seeking shall almost certainly have the immature and irrational behaviors. It is also the case that this entity, as well as almost all seekers, has done substantial work within the framework of the incarnative experience and has indeed developed maturity and rationality. That this instrument should fail to see that which has been accomplished and see only that which remains to be accomplished may well be noted. Indeed, any seeker discovering in itself this complex of mental and mental/emotional distortions shall ponder the possible nonefficacy of judgment.

As we approach the second portion of the query, we view the possibility of infringement upon free will. However, we believe we may make reply within the boundaries of the Law of Confusion.

This particular instrument was not trained, nor did it study, nor worked it at any discipline in order to contact Ra. We were able, as we have said many times, to contact this group using this instrument because of the purity of this instrument's dedication to the service of the One Infinite Creator and also because of the great amount of harmony and acceptance enjoyed each by each within the group, this situation making it possible for the support group to function without significant distortion.

We are humble messengers. How can any thought be taken by an instrument as to the will of the Creator? We thank this group that we may speak through it, but the future is mazed. We cannot know whether our geste may, after one final working, be complete. Can the instrument, then, think for a moment that it shall cease in the service of the One Infinite Creator? We ask the instrument to ponder these queries and observations.

Fragment 46

Don's job as a pilot for Eastern Airlines saw him based in Atlanta.

Book V

Commuting to and from Atlanta became more and more wearing on him and reduced the amount of time available for Ra sessions, due to his absence and due to the time needed for him to recover from his weariness when he was home. Thus, in the fall of 1982 we found a house near the airport in Atlanta that we thought we would move to, so Don's commuting time would be reduced. It had previously been inhabited by people who had trafficked in illegal drugs and who had apparently had numerous disharmonious experiences within the dwelling that was to become our new home. These unfortunate experiences by the former tenants had apparently attracted elementals and lower astral entities into the house, which Carla was somewhat able to perceive.

She wanted very much to move into the house because it would have greatly helped Don to be that close to his work. She wanted to buy new carpeting to replace the soiled one, or, failing that, to begin scrubbing the carpet to cleanse the house of the undesirable presences, but the limitations of our budget and her arthritis made that impossible. Thus a blue-ray blockage of communication occurred that, two days later while she was on her daily walk, was entered by our fifth-density, negative friend and enhanced in the magical sense until she was unable to breathe for about thirty seconds. This was symbolic of her inability to talk to Don about what the house needed. Keeping calm during the distress saw her through it, and talking to Don about the house cleared the blockage.

The queries about the malfunctioning tape recorder refer to strange sounds that came from it a few days later, when Carla was trying to record some of her singing to send to a friend.

The last portion of this session returns to the subject of the house next to the airport in Atlanta that was to become our new home. In our personal and fallible opinions, it is from this point that the difficulties that eventually led to Don's death may be traced. When we returned to our home in Louisville from looking at the new home-to-be in Atlanta, we had just walked in the front door when, all of the sudden, a hawk with a wing span of at least 4 feet landed outside our kitchen window, remained for a few moments, and then flew off over the treetops. Carla and I took the appearance of the hawk as a sign confirming the desirability of the house in Atlanta as our new home. Don, however, was not sure that the hawk was a good sign, and he began to doubt whether we should move to the house after all.

I cannot tell you just how sorry I was that the Atlanta "farm" they were talking about here did not work out as a dwelling place for us. In it, Don was just 3 miles from the airport. It was a very nice place, although peculiar in that the house simply ended with no wall between it and the adjoining horse barn. It was less expensive to rent than the place we had in Louisville, it was a milder climate, and there was room for Jim to stretch out and have his own place, and Don and me to do likewise. What foiled it was an attitude of Don's that was deeply characteristic and, I imagine, stemmed from growing up in the Depression. He did not want to spend the money to get the place really clean. The dirtiness of the place was everywhere; it had been neglected for some time, dusted and vacuumed occasionally, but any spills were left as they fell, and there was the slight patina of ground-in dirt that only good soap would get, and much hard scrubbing. The most logical solution to me was simply to replace the floor covering throughout the dirtied area. Barring that, hiring a good cleaning agency with professional equipment would have sufficed. Don wished to do neither of these things.

When the hawk flew, and Don took it as a bad omen, that was it. There was no more to discuss, as far as Don was concerned. At that point, as Jim has said, there was a definite shift in Don's peace of mind. He was more concerned about having enough energy to work as a pilot than ever, and yet everything seemed to be too much trouble. When we tried to buy the Louisville house from its owner, there was a $5,000.00 dispute that the owner and Donald developed that put the quietus on that deal. So we had to move somewhere, as the owner of the Louisville property was selling it out from under us. Don eventually OK'd a lovely and pricey house on Lake Lanier, about 40 bad miles from the airport. What we hadn't realized was that Atlanta traffic is terrible; after the Olympics were held there, the whole nation became aware of that. And Don had to drive from the extreme north of the traffic tangle to the extreme south, where the airport lay. He spent more time getting there from the lake house than he had done from Louisville, since all he had to do in Louisville was take a short drive to the airport and commute for an hour to Atlanta. The driving from the lake was always an hour and a half to two hours, because of the traffic. There simply seemed no relief and no solution at that house. And so began a difficult experience for all three of us, who somehow had no safe place to be.

If Donald had been normal, he would have been talking a good deal about his various fears. But Don was Don, a wonderful, wise, charming, funny, and truly great man, but a unique man who had from an early age pretended he had no preferences and was only an observer. After his death I found out that he was developing real fears about losing me to Jim. But to me he said nothing, following his usual practice of behaving as though he had no preferences. So I was utterly confused. I figured he was just upset about having the right place, and spent countless hours poring over newspaper ads trying to find him a place he felt good about, but to no avail. From this point on, we were never at peace. And little by little, I realized at a deep level that something serious was going wrong with Don. He began acting *very unlike himself, being unwilling to leave my presence to the point of listening to my music rehearsals, watching me exercise, sleeping in my room; all things the usual Don would scorn. I did not take these things as positive, for I truly loved the irascible and indifferent Don and longed to have him back.*

I was grieving for Donald for months while he was still alive, for he quickly changed to the point that neither I nor he himself could recognize him. This was a time of the most profound distress for Don and for me. Jim was deeply concerned about both of us but was pretty stable. Both Don and I went rather quickly beyond the bounds of normalcy. I suffered a breakdown. I asked for and got help from family, friends, and therapists. So I walked through my nervous breakdown, continuing to function at a basic level. Don suffered a breakdown also, but his came with a real break from reality, and he was in a place where it seemed no one, most of all I, could help him.

Session 96,
September 9, 1982

QUESTIONER: Could you tell me the cause of the lessening of the physical and vital energies?

RA: I am Ra. We found the need of examining the mental configurations of the instrument before framing an answer, due to our reluctance to infringe upon its free will. Those concepts relating to the spiritual contemplation of personal catalyst have been appreciated by the entity, so we may proceed.

This entity has an habitual attitude which is singular; that is, when there is some necessity for action, the entity is accustomed to analyzing the catalyst in terms of service and determining a course. There was a most unusual variation in this configuration of attitude when this instrument beheld the dwelling which is to be inhabited by this group. The instrument perceived those elementals and beings of astral character of which we have spoken. The instrument desired to be of service by achieving the domicile in question but found its instincts reacting to the unwelcome presences. The division of mind configuration was increased by the continuing catalyst of lack of control. Had this entity been able to physically begin cleansing the dwelling, the, shall we say, opening would not have occurred.

Although this entity attempted clear communication upon this matter, and although each in the support group did likewise, the amount of blue-ray work necessary to uncover and grasp the nature of the catalyst was not affected. Therefore, there was an opening quite rare for this mind/body/spirit complex, and into this opening the one which greets you moved and performed what may be considered to be the most potent of its purely magical manifestations to this present nexus, as you know time.

It is well that this instrument is not distorted towards what you may call hysteria, for the potential of this working was such that had the instrument allowed fear to become greater than the will to persevere when it could not breathe, each attempt at respiration would have been even more nearly impossible until the suffocation occurred which was desired by the one which greets you in its own way. Thus the entity would have passed from this incarnation.

QUESTIONER: Does this threat, shall I say, still exist, and, if so, is there something that we can do to alleviate it?

RA: I am Ra. This threat no longer exists, if you wish to phrase this greeting in this manner. The communication which was affected by the scribe and then by the questioner did close the opening and enable the instrument to begin assimilating the catalyst it had received.

QUESTIONER: Was the unusual sound on the instrument's tape recorder that occurred while she was trying to record her singing a greeting from our fifth-density, negative associate?

RA: I am Ra. No. Rather it was a greeting from a malfunctioning electronic machine.

QUESTIONER: There was no catalyst for that machine to malfunction from any of the negative entities then. Is that right? It was only a function of the random malfunction of the machine. Am I correct?

RA: I am Ra. No.

QUESTIONER: What was the origin of this malfunction?

RA: I am Ra. There are two difficulties with the machine. Firstly, this instrument has a strong effect upon electromagnetic and electronic machines and instruments, and likely, if continued use of these is desired, should request that another handle the machines. Also, there was some difficulty from physical interference due to the material you call tape catching upon adjoining, what you would call, buttons when the "play" button, as you call it, is depressed.

QUESTIONER: How is Ra able to know all of this information? This is somewhat of an unimportant question, but it is just amazing to me that Ra is able to know all of these trivial things. What do you do, move in time/space and inspect the problem, or what?

RA: I am Ra. Your former supposition is correct; your latter, unintelligible to us.

QUESTIONER: You mean that you move in time/space and inspect the situation to determine the problem. Is that correct?

RA: I am Ra. This is so.

QUESTIONER: Was there a significance with respect to the hawk that landed the other day just outside the kitchen window?

RA: I am Ra. This is correct. We may note that we find it interesting that queries offered to us are often already known. We assume that our confirmation is appreciated.

QUESTIONER: This seems to be connected with the concept of the bird being messengers in the tarot, and this was a demonstration of this concept. I was wondering about the mechanics, you might say, of this type of message. I assume that the hawk was a messenger, and I assume that as I thought of the possible meaning of this with respect to our activities, I was, in the state of free will, getting a message in the appearance of this very unusual bird, unusual, I say, in that it came so close. I would be very interested to know the origin of the message. Would Ra comment on this, please?

RA: I am Ra. No.

QUESTIONER: I was afraid that you would say that. Am I correct in assuming that this is the same type of communication as depicted in Card Number Three of the Catalyst of the Mind?

RA: I am Ra. We may not comment due to the Law of Confusion. There is an acceptable degree of confirmation of items known, but when the recognized subjective sigil[2] is waved and the message not clear, then it is that we must remain silent.

Fragment 47

After more thought on the subject of the hawk, Don again queried Ra about its significance. Since Ra did not wish to infringe upon Don's free will by clearly explaining the meaning of the hawk—and thus making Don's decision to move or not move to the house for him—the most Ra could do was speak in an indirect sense, in a kind of riddle that required that Don, and each of us, make our own determinations. The extreme desire on the part of any positive entities such as Ra to maintain the free will of each person on our third-density planet is due to the fact that if an entity such as Ra gives information that could change one's future choices, that entity, then, has not only taught the third-density being but has learned for it. By learning for it, it has removed the spiritual strength that comes to one who struggles and finally learns for him/herself. In the larger view, this is not seen as a service but as a disservice. Because of Don's doubt about the appropriateness of the house in Atlanta as our next home, we did not move to that house but remained in Louisville for another year. It was the fall of 1983 before we finally found another house in the Atlanta area and moved there. By that time, Don's weariness had increased to the critical point, and he had begun worrying more and more about whether he was even going to have a job since Eastern Airlines was rapidly failing financially.

Ah, to be able to read aright the little hints that the Creator always seems to be offering us! Both Jim and I thought the hawk was simply a confirmation of that location. But Don was the boss and he really felt unsure, to the point that he left, for a time, the idea of moving completely and tried to purchase the house we were renting. As I mentioned, the difference of about 4 percent of the house's cost was in dispute, and Donald did not see his way clear to giving the rather greedy owner an extra bonus for having us over the barrel of "buy or move." So in the end, we were forced to move somewhere, either in Louisville or Atlanta. It was a fateful move, attended from the beginning by struggles and problems. The sad tale of our demise as a group able to contact Ra was beginning.

Session 97,
September 15, 1982

QUESTIONER: I've been doing some consideration of the appearance of the hawk and have made this analysis of the bird in Card Number Three. The bird is a message from the Higher Self, and the position of the wings on Card Three, one pointing toward the female, indicates that it is a message to the female acting as catalyst for the mind. The position of the downward wing indicates that the message is of a negative nature or of a nature indicating the inappropriateness of certain mental activity or plans. Would Ra comment on that?

RA: I am Ra. No.

QUESTIONER: Is the reason for this lack of comment the first distortion?

RA: I am Ra. This is correct.

QUESTIONER: I have analyzed the hawk that I saw immediately after returning from the house in Atlanta as a message, probably from my Higher Self, indicating that the plan of moving was not the best or not too appropriate, since, without the hawk, we would have continued as planned with no added catalyst. This single catalyst of a remarkable nature then, logically, from my point of view, could only mean that there was a message as to the inappropriateness of the plan for some reason yet to be discovered. Would Ra comment on that?

RA: I am Ra. We tread as close as possible to the Law of Confusion in suggesting that not all winged creatures have an archetypical meaning. We might suggest that the noticing of shared subjectively notable phenomena is common when, in another incarnational experience, work significant to the service of increased polarity has been shared. These subjectively interesting shared phenomena then act as a means of communication, the nature of which cannot be discussed by those outside of the shared incarnational experience without the interference with the free will of each entity involved in the complex of subjectively meaningful events.

QUESTIONER: Can Ra tell us the source of the unusual odor in this room this morning?

RA: I am Ra. There are two components to this odor. One is, as has been surmised, the decomposing physical vehicle of one of your second-density rodentia. The second is an elemental which is attempting to take up residence within the putrefying remains of this small creature.

The cleansing of the room and the burning of the incense has discouraged the elemental. The process of decomposition shall, in a short period of your space/time, remove the less than harmonious sensations provided for the nose.

QUESTIONER: I find myself presently in a difficult position of decision, primarily because of the appearance of the aforementioned hawk upon our return from Atlanta. The only objective of any value at all is the work that we are doing, which includes not only the contact but communication and dissemination of this material to those who might request it. Since a move was connected with that, and since the hawk was, to me, obviously a function of that process, I am presently in a quandary with respect to the optimal situation, since I have not yet definitely decided on the significance of the hawk or the advantages or the efficaciousness of the move and do not want to create any process which is basically irreversible if it is going to result in a lack of our ability to be of service to those who would seek that which we are able to manifest in our efforts. Would Ra comment on that situation?

RA: I am Ra. The questioner presumes much, and to comment is an infringement upon its free will. We may suggest the pondering of our previous comments regarding the winged creatures of which you speak. We repeat that any place of working, properly prepared by this group, is acceptable to Ra. The discrimination of choice is yours.

Fragment 48
Session 98 is presented in total here. Our experiences were beginning to become a little more unusual and difficult at this point in our lives. We had difficulty agreeing on how to proceed concerning the house near the airport in Atlanta, and this is the difficulty of blue-ray blockage that Ra speaks of in the very long response to Carla's compound question. Since our difficulties were freely chosen by us, they were fair game for our negative companion of fifth density to intensify.

In querying about how once again to aid our longtime pet and companion, Gandalf, in another tumor-removal operation, we found that second-density creatures are also subject to causing cancer by creating unresolved anger within themselves—the same process that applies for third-density beings.

And, finally, we found when one constructs the artifacts, clothing, or structures with which one accomplishes service-to-others work, there is a great investment of love and magical potential that may result from such homemade and heart-made artifacts.

As we prepare this personal material for publication, I am sitting at the computer and am very tempted to rub my eyes, because the gardening I did earlier placed me in one of many environments to which I'm allergic. I think these allergies are often a complaint of Wanderers and have to do at least partially with the mismatch of vibrations between this earth world and the world of origin. Often the more uncomplaining the Wanderer, the more the body shall act out the difficulties we may have emotionally and mentally with the vibrations here. Certainly this is true of myself. I do see the psychosomatic nature of these allergies and by long practice have developed a fair resistance to them, which allows me to do some of the too many things I enjoy, whether it be patting the cats or pulling henbit out of the ivy. Or eating one of many foods, or dusting, or getting the mold out of something I find at church on one of my housekeeping forays. I doubt I could duck these no matter what my attitude, but I hope they are as little a part of my awareness as possible, and feel that the attitude really is key.

What it shows me is just how carefully balanced we are, as we come into incarnation here. I was given just these distortions, largely in order that I would have plenty of forced time to become more contemplative. It may seem that I am a thoroughgoing mystic, and certainly during many years of forced stillness, I have always found a depth of faith and a joy that illumined my life from within. It is almost as though the adversity of illness or limitation is a teacher, taking you out of the old ways of doing and introducing you to the contemplative life. I have wanted to be here every day of my life, with the exception of some sorry time during early puberty when I lost all faith and decided if I couldn't be of help to anyone, I might as well go on. Which my body obligingly did not six months later, throwing itself into kidney failure brought on by an allergic reaction. And the allergies are there because of the mismatch in vibratory complexes. See how neatly this works. Such is catalyst. It's a wonderful world.

As I got up from the sickbed at last during 1992, I vowed not to lose this love of stillness. But I also love to do, busy bee that I am. Of course I love to help L/L Research with correspondence and writing and channeling, and my church and singing. These are like the footers for the building I live in, real pillars of renewing spirit within. But there's more. I love the company of women and go out of my way to have that gal's night out in my schedule. I love to cook and do as much as I can cram in, and an extension of that is that I take a morning each week to go through the parish where I worship in community and just go around straightening, washing out, putting away, and making ready, especially in the church kitchen but really all over the building. It is a joy being a servant in the Lord's house! And I could continue till you were exhausted of any possible interest. There are so many good things to do, so many needs I hear and wish to respond to. Too many to accomplish, sadly. The plight of the nineties: no time!

What this is all in aid of is simply to demonstrate how deeply bred in the bone my love of helpful activity is. Activity at whatever level I can accomplish it is inevitable. It is part of who I am, and some would say that is a born martyr. Perhaps this is somewhat true. I only know we live and then we are gone, and while I am here, I want to respond as deeply as I can. This means I am always pushing the envelope, and always prey to psychic greeting. I have not ceased being greeted. It is just that I deal with it, as does Jim, with respect, in acknowledging it, and discipline, in allowing it to pass quickly without judgment, knowing the negative essence behind it as part of myself that I love. Acceptance and forgiveness simply move the situation forward, and the crises pass. This is hard-won wisdom. I encourage any groups who get into a situation where psychic greeting is occurring to study the ways of forgiveness and acceptance of this seemingly opposing energy. In claiming the higher truth that all is one, we place ourselves in that finer, fuller light, and the difficulties ease away as we simply persevere in living without fear of these greetings. For those who might be interested, I do have a chapter on psychic greeting and psychic self-defense in my Channeling Handbook. The essence of that advice: fear not, and lean on prayer and keeping the self aligned in open-hearted love.

My recovery from the bad throat infection discussed above was accomplished by a six-week course of antibiotics taken with lots of buttermilk, not a substance I enjoy. It did, however, work.

Gandalf was a very special little person. Given to me by an old friend in 1968, he was a kitten when Donald and I began our life together. He adored Don and would play retriever with him, repeatedly fetching the peppermint candy wrappers Don would tie in a little bow-tie and throw, and putting them in Don's shoes, which were always off if he was at home. His devotion was intense. If we were sitting, he was almost always upon one of us. Don loved to walk around with Gandalf hanging over his shoulder, and I can still see them clearly, doing their daily tour of the rooms of our apartment. Gandalf expressed such love! As he became quite old, he got both arthritis and cancer, but until the moment he died, he was fiercely determined to be here and as close to us as possible. I feel that he has now reincarnated in our beautiful cat "Mo," who expresses much the same energy. I am thankful we have had more time with this soul, who is certainly harvestable to third density.

Session 98 (in total),
September 24, 1982

RA: I am Ra. I greet you in the love and in the light of the One Infinite Creator. We communicate now.

QUESTIONER: Could you first please give me the condition of the instrument?

RA: I am Ra. The physical-energy deficit has somewhat increased. The vital energy distortions are somewhat improved.

QUESTIONER: We eliminated our meditation prior to the session. Would Ra comment on that?

RA: I am Ra. The purpose of preparation for a working is the purification of each entity involved with the working. The removal of a portion of this preparation has a value determined by the purity of each which takes part in the working has achieved without that particular aid.

QUESTIONER: I had just taken a wild guess that possibly it was during that meditation prior to the working that was used by our fifth-density, negative friend to create the allergic reactions and other reactions in the instrument. Was I correct in that assumption, or was I incorrect?

RA: I am Ra. This entity greets the instrument as close to the working in your space/time continuum as is practicable. The elimination of that preparation caused the fifth-density entity to greet this instrument at this juncture of decision not to meditate. The greeting does not take what you would call a noticeable amount of your time.

QUESTIONER: Was the greeting as effective as it would have been if meditation had been done?

RA: I am Ra. Yes.

QUESTIONER: I have a question from the instrument. It states: "Could Ra tell us what factors are allowing our fifth-density, negative companion to be able to continue greeting the instrument in the throat area, as well as with other unusual sensations such as dizziness, the smelling of orange blossoms, the feeling of stepping on imaginary creatures, and what can be done to lessen these greetings? Also, why do the greetings occur on walks?"

RA: I am Ra. There are various portions of the query. We shall attempt answer to each. We tread close to the Law of Confusion, saved only by the awareness that given lack of information, this instrument would, nonetheless, continue to offer its service.
  The working of your fifth-density companion which still affects the instrument was, as we have stated, a potent working. The totality of those biases which offer to the instrument opportunities for increased vital and physical strength, shall we say, were touched by the

working. The blue-ray difficulties were not entirely at an end after the first asking. Again, this group experienced blockage rare for the group; that is, the blue-ray blockage of unclear communication. By this means the efficacy of the working was reinforced.

The potential of this working is significant. The physical exercising, the sacred music, the varieties of experience, and indeed simple social intercourse are jeopardized by a working which attempts to close the throat and the mouth. It is to be noted that there is also the potential for the loss of this contact.

We suggest that the instrument's allergies create a continuous means whereby the distortion created by the magical working may be continued. As we have stated, it shall be necessary, in order to remove the working, to completely remove the distortion within the throat area caused by this working. The continuous aggravation of allergic reactions makes this challenging.

The orange blossom is the odor which you may associate with the social memory complex of fifth-density positive, which is known to you as sound vibration Latwii. This entity was with the instrument as requested by the instrument. The odor was perceived due to the quite sensitive nature of the instrument, due, again, to its, shall we say, acme in the eighteen-day cycle.

The sensation of stepping upon the small animal and killing it was a greeting from your fifth-density, negative companion also made possible by the above circumstance.

As to the removal of the effects of the magical working, we may make two suggestions, one immediate and one general. Firstly, within the body of knowledge which those healers known among your peoples as medical doctors have is the use of harsh chemical substances which you call medicine. These substances almost invariably cause far more changes than are intended in the mind/body/spirit complex. However, in this instance the steroids or, alternately, the antibiotic family might be useful in the complete removal of the difficulty within which the working is still able to thrive. Of course, the allergies would persist after this course of medicine were ended, but the effects of the working would no longer come into play.

The one you call Jerome might well be of aid in this somewhat unorthodox medical situation. As allergies are quite misunderstood by your orthodox healers, it would be inappropriate to subject the instrument to the services of your medical doctors, which find the amelioration of allergic effects to be connected with the intake of these same toxins in milder form. This, shall we say, treats the symptom. However, the changes offered to the body complex are quite inadvisable. The allergy may be seen to be the rejection upon a deep level of the mind complex of the environment of the mind/body/spirit complex. Thus the allergy may be seen in its pure form as the mental/emotional distortion of the deeper self.

The more general recommendation lies with one which does not wish to be identified. There is a code name prayer wheel. We suggest ten treatments from this healer and further suggest a clear reading and subsequent following upon the part of the instrument of the priorities of allergy, especially to your foodstuffs.

Lastly, the effects of the working become apparent upon the walking when the body complex has begun to exert itself to the point of increased respiration. Also a contributing factor is the number of your second-density substances to which this instrument is allergic.

QUESTIONER: Thank you. The second question is "Our oldest cat, Gandalf, has a growth near his spine. Is there anything that makes the surgical removal of this growth less appropriate than the surgical removal of the growth that we had performed a year ago last April, and would the most appropriate action on our part to aid his recovery be the visualization of light surrounding him during the surgery and the repeating of ritual phrases periodically while he is at the veterinarians?"

RA: I am Ra. No. There is no greater cause for caution than previously, and, yes, the phrases of which you speak shall aid the entity. Although this entity is, in body complex, old and therefore liable to danger from what you call your anesthetic, its mental, emotional, and spiritual distortions are such that it is strongly motivated to recover that it might once again rejoin the loved one. Keep in mind that this entity is harvestable third density.

QUESTIONER: Would you explain why you said "Keep in mind that this entity is harvestable third density" and tell me if you have any other specific recommendations with respect to the proposed operation on the growth?

RA: I am Ra. We stated this in order to elucidate our use of the term "spirit complex" as applied to what might be considered a second-density entity. The implications are that this entity shall have far more cause to abide and heal that it may seek the presence of the loved ones.

QUESTIONER: Is there any additional recommendation that Ra could make with respect to the proposed operation?

RA: I am Ra. No.

QUESTIONER: I was wondering if I was correct in my assumption for the reason for the growth was a state of anger in the cat Gandalf, because of the addition of the newer cats in his environment. Was I correct?

RA: I am Ra. The original cause of what you call cancer was the distortion caused by this event. The proximate cause of this growth is the nature of the distortion of the body cells which you call cancer.

QUESTIONER: Are there any other cancerous growths at this time in Gandalf?

RA: I am Ra. Yes.

QUESTIONER: Can we alleviate those and, if so, how and where are they?

RA: I am Ra. None can be alleviated at this space/time nexus. One is located within the juncture of the right hip. Another which is very small is near the organ you call the liver. There are also small cell distortions under the, we may call it, arm, to distinguish the upper appendages, on both sides.

QUESTIONER: Is there anything that we can do to alleviate these problems that are other than surgical to help Gandalf?

RA: I am Ra. Continue in praise and thanksgiving, asking for the removal of these distortions. There are two possible outcomes. Firstly, the entity shall dwell with you in contentment until its physical vehicle holds it no more due to distortions caused by the cancerous cells. Secondly, the life path may become that which allows the healing. We do not infringe upon free will by examining this life path, although we may note the preponderance of life paths which use some distortion such as this to leave the physical body, which in this case is the orange-ray body.

QUESTIONER: Does the cat Fairchild have any of these same type of problems?

RA: I am Ra. Not at this space/time nexus.

QUESTIONER: Was it necessary for the cat Gandalf to be a mind/body/

spirit complex and harvestable third density to have the anger result in cancer?

RA: I am Ra. No.

QUESTIONER: Then any mind/body complex can develop cancer. Is this correct?

RA: I am Ra. This is correct.
At this time we would break our routine by making an observation. We observe the following coincidence. Firstly, the congestion of this instrument's throat due to the flow of mucous caused by energized allergic reaction has, at this point, become such that we may safely predict the probability/possibility vortex approaching certainty that within one-half of an hour we shall need to depart from this working. Secondly, as we noted above, the sound vibration made by one of your sound vibration recording devices was audible to us. If this group desires, it may choose to have sessions which are brought to an ending soon after this sound vibration occurs. This decision would ensure the minimal distortions within the instrument towards the discomfort/comfort within the throat until the effects of the magical working of your fifth-density companion have been removed.

QUESTIONER: That is perfectly fine with us. That noise occurs at the forty-five-minute time period, since the tapes are forty-five minutes on a side. I would just ask as the final question, then, if the new table that Jim has built for the appurtenances is satisfactory to hold them, since it will give us more room to walk around the bed, and is it better to leave it in its natural condition, or is it better to coat it with linseed oil, varnish, or paint?

RA: I am Ra. We view this appurtenance. It sings with joy. The pine vibrates in praise. Much investment of this working in wood has been done. It is acceptable. We may suggest it be left either as it is or rubbed with the oil, which also is easily magnetized and holds the proffered vibration to a profound extent.

QUESTIONER: I was wondering if this would be an appropriate time to end since the tape recorder clicked some time ago.

RA: I am Ra. This is a matter for your discrimination. The instrument remains open to our use, although, as we have noted, the physical distortions begin to mount.

QUESTIONER: Then we had better close to protect the instrument's physical energy, and I will ask if there is anything that we can do to improve the contact or to make the instrument more comfortable?

RA: I am Ra. All is well. We find your concerns appropriate.

We leave you in the love and in the light of the One Infinite Creator. Go forth, therefore, rejoicing in the power and in the peace of the One. Adonai.

Fragment 49

Most people would probably not have described the feeling of not quite being whole and in harmony that our group experienced during the fall of 1982 as true disharmony. Yet, as one moves further along the path of seeking light and begins to stand closer to it, as we were privileged to do in the Ra contact, even the smallest of lapses of harmony, when left unresolved, can become targets of opportunity for those such as our friend of negative polarity to intensify. These psychic greetings can become great opportunities to heal those lapses of harmony and to move even further and faster upon the evolutionary journey, because what such a negative entity is actually doing when it intensifies one's disharmonious choices is pointing out to you weak points that you might have missed in your own conscious seeking. But one must take quick and thorough action in order to unravel these distortions in one's beingness or further confusion and difficulty may ensue, again due to, first, your original free-will choice; second, the intensification of that choice by the negative entity; and, third, by lack of attention on your part in finally resolving the distortion and balancing it. Fortunately, most people do not have to deal with the magical abilities of a fifth-density entity but with the lesser abilities of the fourth-density minions, who are usually quite effective on their own.

Thus as Carla was finally getting rid of the effects of the intensification of her blue-ray blockage concerning renting and then cleaning the house next to the airport in Atlanta, I began to notice an increase in my pre-incarnatively chosen distortion of anger/frustration. Notice the fundamental principle in Ra's first sentence in response to my question. All of our distortions and thus all of our learning are the result of the limitation of the viewpoint. We limit our points of view consciously or unconsciously, pre-incarnatively or during the incarnation, in order to gain a certain bias that may then draw unto it the opposite bias and offer us the opportunity for balance. By being able to see each bias as an opportunity for the Creator to know Itself and for us to know ourselves as the Creator, we more and more become able to accept ourselves. We become able to find love and acceptance not only in ourselves but in others who share our characteristics, and our viewpoint is widened by our efforts to learn and to serve. Such growth is not possible without biases or distortions, and these biases and distortions are not possible without the choice to limit the viewpoint in one way or another. So we determine what lessons and services we shall attempt during any incarnation by the way in which we limit our viewpoint.

Another interesting point to note here is that whatever one's basic nature is, whether it be love, wisdom, power, or some blend of these three, one does well to express that nature in a regularized fashion. So does one become a channel for it, not by holding on to it but by giving it away.

Again, we see another purpose of anger or the opportunity that it might present to one expressing it. Being the polar opposite of love, it may attract that love and compassion to the person feeling it. Remorse and sorrow often attract love and compassion to a positive seeker who has experienced a great deal of anger. Anger may also be seen as the negative expression of power; that is, destruction and separation, with the positive side being construction and unification. So it is not necessary to repress or overcome qualities in our being that seem negative and hurtful, but, rather, to see them as potentials for achieving balance. When these negative qualities are followed to their source, they can enable the seeker to take advantage of the opportunities for knowing the self, the Creator, and the creation as portions of a complete unity. Ra's last sentence underscores this point.

I have thought that this particular fragment is perhaps the best example in this current volume of why Ra can be so helpful. We three humans were doing our level best to stay totally harmonized in movement and rhythm, but we often erred, as do all of us, no matter what, if not today then tomorrow. This is the human estate. Working on this catalyst between us with an intensity born of wishing to remain clear enough to contact Ra, we developed questions for Ra, trying to get more of a bead on what our distortions were, and how to approach seating these incoming catalysts. But no question, however cleverly phrased, could expect to garner a piece of advice like "as in all distortions, the source is the limit of the viewpoint." In terms of the old saw about a choice between giving a man a fish and giving him a pole and teaching him fishing, Ra always went for the fishing pole, plus bait. And all without infringement on free will: an impressive task, and appreciated by us. We pored over these little comments a lot. They really did help us focus.

I've already talked about the buttermilk/penicillin cure. The principle Ra followed in OK'ing my wearing of a little cross in sessions seems very telling for a lot of questions we have about whether we should do something or not. They said it wasn't the greatest in terms of what complications it would cause, but it was OK because it was a symbol that strengthened me in a real way. This concept of balance and the strength of being as flowing into a pattern that is read as metaphysical rather than physical is a real help to people who want to be less allergic or depressed or whatever: do what feels right, letting the mystical meaning have as much importance as the physical. Find the balance.

Ra's advice to Jim struck home both to Jim and to Don and me. After we read this, we decided to encourage Jim to take the afternoon for solitude. He really enjoyed, and still enjoys, this routine, going out into the gardens for whatever needs doing after lunch and finishing up at eventide with a bath. I am often out there with him, but I do leave him in solitude unless I have a gardening question. To watch Jim work is to understand the power and purpose of ritual and magic.

My dear Mick (I call him that to distinguish him from my brother and also from my first husband, both named Jim) still has an amazingly bright and fiery temper. I stand in awe, quite literally, and watch it sweep through him like a tornado. He has, through the years, found ways to behave less angrily, but that core imbalance for him runs very deep, rather like my wanting to do too much. Some things about all of us are far from smart, but when you try to eradicate them, they just snicker! Nope—we're part of the package, they seem to say. I have worked my way through the substantial catalyst this has been for me, and give Mick thanks for such excellent catalyst. I have never been hurt physically, mind you. This is a solo act. I now simply observe and accept. I know it only seems that way. I affirm perfection. That is what I have learned to do so far, both to my own humanity and other people's. Meanwhile, he has had to learn to tend me rather like a shepherd, walking along and picking up the things I drip behind me as I go absentmindedly on. No one gets away free!

I can only say that meditation and a daily offering each day as a beginning help for me. They are the basis of my day, and I think Jim would also say that. So I encourage any who might have had trouble doing that to try again. This time, adapt the practice to your life. It is a routine that has served us well. Perhaps that is too much for you, but you see how to build a time for you and the Creator to meet. You can't just remake your life around a newly discovered devotional or mystic aspect of yourself; you have to practice a rule of life that gives you time to do your necessaries. I think that one quick drink is a powerful thing. So please try again, if you have given up. For those who want to read about meditation, I recommend Joel Goldsmith's little book, The Art of Meditation.

Session 99,
November 18, 1982

QUESTIONER: What are the foodstuffs that are creating this allergic reaction?

RA: I am Ra. That which you call the buttermilk, though appropriately used in the healing work undertaken for the throat and chest areas, is the substance to which the entity has allergy.

QUESTIONER: The instrument asked if she could keep the small gold cross on while she is in one of these sessions. Will that cause any distortion in these workings?

RA: I am Ra. We scan the mental distortions of the instrument. Although the presence of the metallic substance is, in general, not recommended, in this instance, as we find those distortions weakening the mental/emotional complex of the instrument due to its empathic distortions, the figure is specifically recommended for use by this instrument. We would request that should any strengthening be done to the chain, as we find intended by this instrument, the strengthening links which symbolize eternity to this instrument be as high in purity or higher than the remainder of the device.

In this nexus that which this device represents to this instrument is a much-needed strengthener of the mental/emotional patterns which have been much disrupted from the usual configuration of distortions.

QUESTIONER: Is there anything further that needs to be done by or for the instrument to remove the magical working, or any of its after-effects, in her throat area by our fifth-density, negative companion?

RA: I am Ra. No.

QUESTIONER: Finally, I have a question from Jim, stating: "For the last two weeks I have often found myself on the edge of anger and frustration, have had a nearly constant dull pain in the area of my indigo-ray center, and have felt quite drained of energy. Would Ra comment on the source of these experiences and any thoughts or actions that might alleviate them?"

RA: I am Ra. As in all distortions, the source is the limit of the viewpoint. We may, without serious infringement, suggest three courses of behavior which shall operate upon the distortion expressed.

Firstly, it would be well for the scribe to engage, if not daily then as nearly so as possible, in a solitary strenuous activity which brings this entity to the true physical weariness. Further, although any activity may suffice, an activity chosen for its intended service to the harmony of the group would be quite efficacious.

The second activity is some of your space/time and time/space taken by the entity, directly or as nearly so as possible to the strenuous activity, for solitary contemplation.

Thirdly, the enthusiastic pursuit of the balancing and silent meditations cannot be deleted from the list of helpful activities for this entity.

We may note that the great forte of the scribe is summed in the inadequate sound vibration complex power. The flow of power, just as the flow of love or wisdom, is enabled not by the chary[3] conserver of its use but by the constant user. The physical manifestation of power being either constructive or destructive strenuous activity, the power-filled entity must needs exercise that manifestation. This entity experiences a distortion in the direction of an excess of stored energy. It is well to know the self and to guard and use those attributes which the self has provided for its learning and its service.

Fragment 50

In the material from Session 100, note how the limit of the viewpoint changes the nature of the answer. Carla's tendency toward martyrdom, seen from the time/space or metaphysical point of view, is quite helpful in her own evolutionary process. But that same tendency, seen from the space/time or physical point of view, is seen as a tendency that may present difficulties for the services that one wishes to offer during the incarnation.

I had a very hard time with the "swirling waters" from the start; immersed in that high tub, just big enough to fold myself into, I had to tolerate levels up around my mouth in order for the water to beat on my upper back and neck, which were where the worst of the joints of my spine were. All the claustrophobia I had ever felt was squared by this exercise. It was as much an act of will and faith as a physical practice. I did find it very comforting. At the time, I was so small, wearing preteen sizes and weighing around 80–85, that I had to wear a weight to hold myself down on the floor of the specially made tub; otherwise I floated around. I would have no such trouble now, as change of life has rendered me a larger and more mature-looking being. Jim says I used to be a little angel and now I am a cherub. So I could probably endure this better now. But I find that Jim's massages are the best thing. Water is wonderful, but the healing power of touch cannot be over-rated.

Shortly after we acquired this therapy tub, I was struck with a sudden and dramatic frenzy of fear. I bolted out of the tub and found myself cowering on the back of one of the sofas, growling at Jim and Don. At the time I thought it was a psychic greeting, but later Ra confirmed that Don and I had just made a deleterious and complete unity/exchange of our mental and emotional natures, and I was experiencing for the first time the degree of alienation and real fear with which he saw this quarrelsome world. He really, really had trouble living on this earth, although one would never have known it from gazing at him. Don was always infinitely cool. But beneath that calm surface was a really difficult and challenging amount of imbalance. How he managed to live here as long as he did is perhaps beyond me to know.

Session 100,
November 29, 1982

QUESTIONER: The instrument asks if there is some problem with the swirling waters, since she feels very dizzy after each application. Could Ra comment on that, please?

RA: I am Ra. Yes.

QUESTIONER: Would Ra please comment?

RA: I am Ra. As has been previously noted, the instrument has the propensity for attempting to exceed its limits. If one considers the metaphysical or time/space aspect of an incarnation, this is a fortunate and efficient use of catalyst, as the will is constantly being strengthened, and, further, if the limitations are exceeded in the service of others, the polarization is also most efficient.

However, we perceive the query to speak to the space/time portion of incarnational experience and in that framework would again ask the instrument to consider the value of martyrdom. The instrument may examine its range of reactions to this swirling waters. It will discover a correlation between it and other activity. When the so-called aerobic exercise is pursued no less than three of your hours, and preferably five of your hours, should pass betwixt it and the swirling waters. When the walking has been accomplished, a period of no less than, we believe, forty of your minutes must needs transpire before the swirling waters, and preferably twice that amount of your space/time.

It is true that some greeting has encouraged the dizziness felt by the instrument. However, its source is largely the determination of the instrument to remain immersed in swirling waters past the period of space/time it may abide therein without exceeding its physical limits.

Fragment 51

In Session 101 I got an excellent opportunity to work on my anger/frustration distortion again. This time, however, it was not pointed only at myself. This "negative wisdom" was pointed at Don over a period of two days when it was time to have Books II and III reprinted. Don wanted to put all of the books—I, II, and III—into one book instead. It didn't matter that that was impossible due to lack of money to do it the way Don wanted to do it—typeset and hardback. What mattered was that I allowed a disharmony to result that went unresolved for two days. This became an excellent opportunity for our friend of negative fifth density to magnify the difficulty, and the means by which this was done proved to be quite interesting, especially to me, when I developed a rare kidney disease. It was called lipoid nephritis or minimal change syndrome, and soon I had gained about 30 pounds of water weight as a result of it. The last sentence in the first paragraph of Ra's response seems to us to be the key concept in this particular incident. The last two sentences in that response are interesting in their general application to all seekers.

You will note toward the middle of this session that another house in Atlanta is mentioned as a possible location for our group. We were still hoping to get closer to Don's work so that there would be less strain on him in getting to his job. Later, we found a third house, which will be mentioned in Session 105, and it was this house that we eventually moved to in November 1983.

The next-to-the-last question concerns another instrument who had reported difficulties with her body swelling much as mine had done. Don asked if there were any way that we could give her information about her condition, since we had just talked to her on the phone to compare the swelling in the ranks of our two groups. The first paragraph of Ra's response lays out the general principle that affects all individuals and groups doing work of a more intensive service-to-others nature. The second paragraph of Ra's response refers to the situation in which that particular instrument worked, but the general application of those concepts is obvious.

The combination of healing approaches found my condition in remission within six months.

I wish you could have seen the look on Dr. Stewart Graves's face when that worthy reviewed Ra's diagnosis. He carefully looked up the known causes of Jim's variety of kidney disease and found that insect bites and the allergic reaction to them were a rarely found but duly noted cause of the condition. In the absence of any other possible cause, it was recorded an allergic reaction. Oddly, when I experienced kidney failure as a teenager, allergic reaction was also the doctor's best guess as to cause.

By this time, it may seem to you that psychic greetings were really occupying our time. You would be right. As Jim and Ra both say, it is easier to be noticed when you're standing in a spotlight. Metaphysically, the contact with those of Ra was a blinding cynosure. Although we continued to be obscure and completely anonymous in any earthly sense, we had become very noticeable to "the loyal opposition."

To my mind, the fatal weakness of our group was its humanity, in dealing with threeness. Although in fact our consciously known energies were in perfect harmony and agreement, there were human distortions from below the level of conscious control that allowed a wedge to be driven in between Don and me, so he lost faith in "us." When he began experiencing this profound depression, which seemed to over-take him at a crawling, yet inexorable pace, his utter disdain for any opinion but his own did not stand him in good stead. This was the beginning of a pattern that in the end turned fatal and ended my beloved companion's life, and dear Ra's contact with our group.

Does this constitute a suggestion that a group should not work unless the energies are two by two, and only couples can join in? Not specifically, I do not think, but it is certainly something to ponder. Could we have done better? After years of the Joycean "agenbite of inwit," I still do not think we could have. Our behavior was at all times a true manifestation of ourselves. In no wise did either Jim or myself ever even think to change the relationship with each other, or with Donald. And Don had ever kept his own counsel, and there was no hope that he would come to me or Jim and tell us what worries he had in his mind and heart.

Further, when any group works and lives together, regardless of whether the number is paired or singles are mixed in, there will always be human error in the manifested life of each, and to the extent that people's distortions and fears have a dynamic, there will be misunderstandings and confusion, pulling back and apart from total trust. So it behooves all those working with the light, hoping to be a positive influence on the planetary consciousness, to communicate at once those fears and doubts that might pile up inside. If we had ever been able to talk with total openness, Don and I, I think I could have set his mind at ease. But Don would not have been himself if he had done so. Nor would I have been myself if I had somehow known Don was doubting my fidelity. Being within my self, I cannot imagine, either then or now, anyone thinking that I would be disloyal or untrue to any agreement. I have never done that in this incarnation.

Ultimately, one looks at such a pickle as we got into, and knows its utter perfection and inevitability. I have and will always think of Don, my B.C., every hour of every day, and his suffering is ever before me. But I no longer feel the keen sorrow that laid me low for the first few years after his death. All is well, nothing is lost. And I can feel the sun on my face this day, without the urge I used to have to stay in the shade and mourn my losses. Time has restored my broken spirit and let my being flow sweetly and rhythmically again. And Donald is right here, within. Interestingly enough, we often get mail saying that Don has helped them, either with something from his work or in an actual visitation. Don's great generosity of spirit, freed from the constrictive hold he had on it when alive, has over-flowed into timelessness, and I think his service will continue as long as there are those who need his special brand of wisdom and depth of soul.

Ra's statement that the source of catalyst is the self, especially the higher self, is profound, I think. We always relate to the pain of new catalyst by relating to the other person as bringer of catalyst. In doing so, we forget that the other is ourselves. Not LIKE ourselves, but our very hearts and souls. In this way of seeing, we can look at the fullness of tragedy in Don's and my illness and his death as the Creator serving the creator with exactly the catalyst needed for the utmost polarization in consciousness and the greatest growth of spirit. In opening his heart, Don fell ill and died, in the tradition of lost love and desperate romance that has moved us since the beginning of history. And that death was an utter giving away of self. It was as though Don finished everything else he wished to do in life and then took on the personal reason he had come to earth's physical plane: the opening of his heart. He was so very wise—and with the sacrifice of self in the most brutal, literal sense, that wisdom was balanced fully with compassion and open-hearted love.

As for me, I cannot fault the path that stubbornly sent my soul to batter against the walls of self until I at last began struggling to express wisdom as well as love in my life. Such were our gifts to each other; such are the currents between us all.

Since Ra gave us the cleansing ritual referred to in this session, I've seen it used several times by those who have come to

L/L Research, and in every case it seems to have been quite useful. I think that doing some sort of cleansing of a new place is a good metaphysical habit, for people do leave behind the thought-forms' traces imprinted on the aura of the places they have been, especially those they've stayed in for considerable time. And even when the vibrations are basically good, they might not harmonize completely with your own. So it is good to magnetize the place for your own uses, even if all you do is burn sage or say a prayer *of dedication. The world of spirit has much to do with us, though we cannot in most ways know or see such influence. Offering that part of things respect is wise.*

Session 101 (in total), December 21, 1982

RA: I am Ra. I greet you in the love and in the light of the One Infinite Creator. We communicate now.

QUESTIONER: Could you first please give me the condition of the instrument?

RA: I am Ra. All energy levels of the instrument are somewhat diminished due to the distortions of physical pain and recent mental/emotional catalyst. However, the energy levels appear to be very liable to be improved in what you call your immediate future.

QUESTIONER: Thank you. What has caused the swelling in Jim's body, and what can be done to heal it?

RA: I am Ra. For the answer to this query we must begin with the consideration of the serpent, signifying wisdom. This symbol has the value of the ease of viewing the two faces of the one who is wise. Positive wisdom adorns the brow indicating indigo-ray work. Negative wisdom, by which we intend to signify expressions which effectually separate the self from the other-self, may be symbolized by poison of the fangs. To use that which a mind/body/spirit complex has gained of wisdom for the uses of separation is to invite the fatal bite of that wisdom's darker side.

The entity has a mental/emotional tendency, which has been lessening in distortion for some of your space/time, towards negative wisdom. The entity's being already aware of this causes us not to dwell upon this point but merely to specifically draw the boundaries of the metaphysical background for the energizing of a series of bites from one of your second-density species. In this case the bite was no more than that of one of the arachnids, sometimes called the wood spider. However, it is possible that were enough work done to test the origin of the pathology of the entity, it is within possibility/probability limits that the testing would show the bite of the cottonmouth rather than the bite of the common wood spider.

The energizing took its place within the lymphatic system of the entity's yellow-ray, physical body. Therefore, the working continues. There is increasing strain upon the spleen, the suprarenal glands, the renal complex, and some possibility/probability of difficulty with the liver. Further, the lymphatic difficulties have begun to strain the entity's bronchial system. This is some general information upon what is to be noted as a somewhat efficient working.

The removal of these distortions has several portions. Firstly, it is well to seek the good offices of the one known as Stuart so that harsh chemical means may be taken to reawaken the histaminic reflexes of the entity and to aid in the removal of edema.

Secondly, we suggest that which has already begun; that is, the request of the one known now to this group as Bob that this entity may focus its aid upon the metaphysical connections with the yellow-ray body.

Thirdly, the entity must take note of its physical vehicle's need for potassium. The ingesting of the fruit of the banana palm is recommended.

Fourthly, the link between the swelling of contumely[4] and the apparent present situation is helpful. As always, the support of the harmonious group is an aid, as is meditation. It is to be noted that this entity requires some discipline in the meditation which the others of the group do not find necessary in the same manner. Therefore, the entity may continue with its forms of meditation, knowing that each in the group supports it entirely although the instinct to share in the discipline is not always present. Each entity has its ways of viewing and learning from the illusion, and each processes catalyst using unique circuitry. Thus, all need not be the same to be equal in will and faith.

QUESTIONER: Thank you. I will make a statement about the way I see the action in this instance and would request Ra's comment on it. I see the present situation as the Creator knowing Itself by using the concept of polarization. We seem to accentuate or to produce catalyst to increase the desired polarization, whether the desired mechanism be random, through what we call the Higher Self, or through utilizing the services of an oppositely polarized entity acting upon us. All of these seem to produce the same effect, which is more intense polarization in the desired direction once that direction has been definitely chosen. I see the catalyst of the second-density insect bite being a function of either or any of the sources of which I have spoken, from random to the Higher Self or polarized services of negative entities who monitor our activities, all of which have roughly the same ultimate effect. Would Ra comment on my observation?

RA: I am Ra. We find your observations unexceptional and, in the large, correct.

QUESTIONER: In this particular case, which avenue was the one that produced the catalyst of the bite?

RA: I am Ra. The nature of catalyst is such that there is only one source, for the catalyst and experience are further attempts at specificity in dealing with the architecture of the unconscious mind of the self. Therefore, in an incarnational experience, the self as Creator, especially the Higher Self, is the base from which catalyst stands to offer its service to the mind, body, or spirit.

In the sense which we feel you intend, the source was the fifth-density, negative friend which had noted the gradual falling away of the inharmonious patterns of the distortion called anger/frustration in the entity. The insect was easily led to an attack, and the physical vehicle, which had long-standing allergies and sensitivities, was also easily led into the mechanisms of the failure of the lymphatic function and the greatly diminished ability of the immune system to remove from the yellow-ray body that which distorted it.

QUESTIONER: Something occurred to me. I am going to make a guess that my illness over the past week was a function of an action by my Higher Self to eliminate the possibility of a residence in the proximity of a large number of bees that I observed. Would Ra comment on my statement?

RA: I am Ra. We can comment, not upon the questioner's physical distortions but upon the indubitable truth of second-density hive creatures; that is, that a hive mentality as a whole can be influenced by one strong metaphysical impulse. Both the instrument and the scribe have the capacity for great distortions toward nonviability, given such an attack by a great number of the stinging insects.

QUESTIONER: Are the thought-form parameters and the general parameters of the 893 Oakdale Road address in Atlanta such that no cleansing would be necessary, if Ra has this information?

RA: I am Ra. No.

QUESTIONER: Would cleansing of the nature suggested for the other house just south of the airport in Atlanta be advisable for the 893 Oakdale Road address?

RA: I am Ra. We note that any residence, whether previously benign, as is the one of which you speak, or previously of malignant character, needs the basic cleansing of the salt, water, and broom. The benign nature of the aforementioned domicile is such that the cleansing could be done in two portions; that is, no egress or entrance through any but one opening for one cleansing. Then egress and entrance from all other places while the remaining portal is properly sealed. The placing of salt may be done at the place which is not being sealed during the first of the cleansings, and the salt may be requested to act as seal and yet allow the passage of gentle spirits such as yourselves. We suggest that you speak to this substance and name each entity for which permission is needed in order to pass. Let no person pass without permission being asked of the salt. This is the case in the residence of which you speak.

QUESTIONER: Thank you. Could Ra give information on any way that we could give information to [name] as to how to alleviate her present condition of swelling?

RA: I am Ra. We may only suggest that the honor of propinquity to light carries with it the Law of Responsibility. The duty to refrain from contumely and discord in all things, which, when unresolved within, makes way for workings, lies before the instrument of which you speak. This entity may, if it is desired by the scribe, share our comments upon the working of the latter entity.

The entity which is given constant and unremitting approval by those surrounding it suffers from the loss of the mirroring effect of those which reflect truthfully rather than unquestioningly. This is not a suggestion to reinstate judgment but merely a suggestion for all those supporting instruments; that is, support, be harmonious, share in love, joy, and thanksgiving, but find love within truth, for each instrument benefits from this support more than from the total admiration which overcomes discrimination.

QUESTIONER: Thank you. That was the forty-five-minute signal, so I will ask if there is anything that we can do to make the instrument more comfortable or to improve the contact.

RA: I am Ra. We find that this instrument has used all the transferred energy and has been speaking using its vital-energy reserve. We do suggest using the transferred sexual energy to the total exclusion of vital reserves if possible.

The alignments are as they must be for all to continue well. We are grateful for the conscientiousness of the support group.

I am Ra. I leave this group glorying in the love and in the light of the One Infinite Creator. Go forth rejoicing, therefore, in the power and in the peace of the Creator. Adonai.

Fragment 52

And now, in Session 102, it was once again Carla's turn to experience another psychic greeting, which intensified a momentary lapse from harmony on her part. She was unable to accept a portion of my perception of our shared relationship for the period of about an hour or two, but that was long enough, due to her intense emotions during that time, for a potent working to be accomplished by our friend of negative polarity. Fortunately, most people will not have to worry about such instant and dramatic intensifications of disharmonious moments, since few people or groups attract the attention of fifth-density, negative entities. But the general principle is that one who is standing close to light experiences an honor that must be balanced by the responsibility of reflecting that light as harmoniously as possible, and this principle holds for all seekers. Failure to live up to that responsibility simply brings one another more intensive opportunity to do so until it is done, or until one steps away from the light.

In the third paragraph of Ra's second response, we find the key concept or attitude for dealing with any such psychic greetings, or any difficulties in general, that one may face in the life patterns. Further into the session, Ra gives the basic criteria for the unblocking of the yellow-ray energy center, the one with which Carla was working in this situation. Surgery was avoided, and the spasming condition of Carla's abdominal region was brought under control over a period of about two years. A potent working, that one!

Ah, humanity! Jim's and my discord was about that age-old dynamic between men and women: monogamy. Who was it that wrote the little ditty "Hogamus, higgimus, men are polygamous; Higgimus, hogamus, dames are monogamous"? Ogden Nash? Dorothy Parker? At any rate, this is true, or tends to be. Jim asked for an open relationship several times in our early days together. Being most honestly more a friend than a BOY-friend, being linked to me primarily by our work together rather than any romantic interest, he naturally responded to the many lovely women who came his way. In this same circumstance, it never occurred to me to seek a further relationship. I was totally satisfied to have Don as my companion and mate and had long since left off blaming him for wanting to be celibate, and also was perfectly happy with Jim's and my friendship and intimate life together. How we do stir up confusion with our desires! Yet to desire is most proper.

I think much of learning in life is involved with the right use of will and desire.

One of the major healings of my life occurred with the removal of about half my descending colon in 1992. This cleared out much old and dead matter and enabled me to do corresponding work within myself at the metaphysical level. There was much to release, and I felt wonderful to be able to do that. The psyche and the soma, soul and body, are inextricably intertwined, and pain to one will be reflected in the other. However, when the body alone is harmed, the mind is much freer to revision the trauma than when it is the mind and emotions that are injured. If such damage is not addressed and respected, it can move ever deeper into the body's health, unbalancing and undermining it.

After that surgery, with its attendant metaphysical work, I had released all I could of the whole tragedy of Don's death and my life, so diminished without his company. And so I became finally able to move on into new life. I was sent home with a new diet, following closely Ra's suggestions. Every look into my GI system showed ulcers, and given my thirty-year use of cortisone, this is not remarkable. The diet was called "low sediment," and on it were the well-cooked meats, veggies and fruits, sugars, and fats that Ra had recommended, but not on it were the usual health foods—whole grains, nuts, berries, uncooked fruits and vegetables. I think one could almost characterize it as the UN-health diet! Yet, it has worked, thank the Lord, for five years so far, and I am most grateful. I think I share with many people who have chronic disease that feeling of living on the razor's edge. I have to be careful, as mistakes are costly. I do miss salads especially but have no argument with the destiny that has allowed me these years of life I almost did not have.

One note about "Bob": he was an amazing help in one area: my feelings of suicidal nature. After Don's death, and especially after I found out what Don had been thinking, I felt totally guilty for not being able to see his fears and allay them. I felt as though it was all my fault. The penalty, I felt strongly, should be death. I was quite unwilling to take my own life. Knowing how it had affected me when Don died, I knew I could never do that to those I love. Which left me hanging between life and death. Through the years from 1984 to 1992, the forces of death circled ever closer until finally I could look death in the eye and find the faith to affirm life and love and healing. The part prayer had in this was substantial to say the least. And Bob's prayers were especially powerful to save. He told me of these suicidal vibrations long before I could do much besides drown in sorrow, and helped me through those pangs of self-knowledge and self-judgment that were so unbalanced. And he was joined by so many others. I had the sensation of being upheld in love, safe and sound, during the whole of the 1991–92 experience, which involved four trips to the hospital, critically ill and quite foundered, my GI tract closed tight.

We have lost touch with Bob, in case you would wish us to give his name and direction. He let us know he had retired from active healing and wished to spend his time now in deep prayer on the planetary level. Our thanks and blessings, wherever you are, dear Bob.

It was not easy to find Arthur Schoen. Ra had pronounced his last name "Shane," but there was not an M.D. of any type by that name. Finally we hit upon the German spelling—although if the name had been pronounced correctly, it would be "shourn," more or less. But this IS America, so of course the name was Americanized. We actually did go see this man but left before he could treat me, as he and Donald did not see eye to eye. This is no surprise, for Don wanted him to read Ra's diagnosis, and the doctor did not really feel comfortable consulting with a discarnate entity.

Ra's suggestion to "link hands and walk towards the sun" is good counsel indeed. Had we been able to dwell in praise and thanksgiving, much would have been altered. But things were as they were. From this remove of time, I see and give praise and thanks for every moment we had together. Whatever it has cost, it was and is worth it all.

Session 102 (in total), March 22, 1983

RA: I am Ra. I greet you in the love and in the light of the One Infinite Creator. We communicate now.

QUESTIONER: Would you first please give me the condition of the instrument?

RA: I am Ra. The physical-energy deficit of this entity is the most substantial across which we have come. The mental and mental/emotional distortions are near to balance, and the vital energy of the instrument, as a whole, is distorted towards health or strength/weakness due to the will of the instrument.

QUESTIONER: Will Ra please tell us what caused the pain and cramping in the instrument's stomach, and what could be done to heal it?

RA: In order to observe the cause of physical distortions towards illness, one must look to the energy center which is blocked. In this situation, the blockage being yellow ray, the experience has had the characteristics of that region of the chemical body. The so-called lacuna in the wind-written armor of light and love was closed and not only repaired but much improved. However, the distortions energized during this momentary lapse from free energy flow are serious and shall be continuing for, in all possibility/probability vortices, some of your space/time, for a predisposition to spasticity in the transverse colon has been energized. There is also preexisting weakness in pancreatic functions, especially that link with the hypothalamus. There is also the preexisting damage to portions of the liver. These lacks or distortions manifest in that portion of the system directly proceeding from the jejunum. Further, there is some irritation closer to the duodenum which causes the instrument to fail in assimilating foodstuffs. This is an allopathically caused irritation.

The diet is of central import. We can go no further in observing the system of the entity, as a full discussion of those distortions towards various weakness/strengths which contribute to the present difficulty begins with the lips and ends with the anus. We may note that the instrument has remained centered upon the Creator at a percentage exceeding 90. This is the key. Continue in thanksgiving and gratitude for all things.

There are stronger antispasmodic drugs which the one not known to this instrument, but known as Arthur, may aid by the offering. The recommendation to do this, being as it is that which does not retain or remove life and does further remove from the instrument its opportunities for study in this situation, needs must be withheld. We are not in a position to recommend treatment at this space/time beyond the watching of the types of foodstuffs ingested.

QUESTIONER: Thank you. I'm not sure that I understood everything that you said. The last name of this Arthur, and where he is located? Can you give me that information?

RA: I am Ra. We can.

QUESTIONER: Will you please do that?

RA: I am Ra. The entity, sound vibration Arthur, has a surname Schoen and is of your locality.

QUESTIONER: What foods should the instrument eliminate in her diet in order to alleviate these painful attacks?

RA: The information gained from the one known as Bob is that which is to be recommended. Further, all foodstuffs are to be cooked so that those things which are ingested be soft and easily macerated. There is a complex addiction, due to long-standing eating habits, to your sugars.

It is to be recommended that, therefore, this sugar be given in its more concentrated form in your time of late afternoon, as you term it, with the ingestion of the sugared libation approximately one to two of your hours after the evening meal. It is further suggested that since this instrument has been using sugars for carbohydrates that a small amount of carbohydrates, low in sugar, be ingested approximately one to two of your hours before the sleeping period.

QUESTIONER: As I understand what you say, the instrument is to have no sugar until late in the afternoon. Is that correct?

RA: I am Ra. No.

QUESTIONER: I didn't fully understand what you meant about when she should have the sugar. Could you clear that up, please?

RA: I am Ra. The concentrated sugar—that is, the dessert, the ice cream, the cookie—should be ingested at that time. Small amounts of the fructose, maple, or raw honey may be ingested periodically for, as we have said, the chemistry of this yellow-ray body is such that the sugar is being used by blood enzymes as would carbohydrates in a less distorted yellow-ray, physical vehicle.

QUESTIONER: I'm sorry that I am so slow at picking up precisely what we are getting at here. I want to be sure that we get this right, so I'll probably ask a few more stupid questions. Was the spasm that caused the extreme pain a spasm of the ileum?

RA: I am Ra. Partially. The transverse colon also spasmed, as did the ducts to the liver in its lower portion. There were also muscle spasms from the bronchial coverings down through the pelvis and from shoulder blades to hips. These sympathetic spasms are a symptom of the exhaustion of the entity's physical vehicle.

QUESTIONER: Then the opening for these spasms was originally made by the yellow-ray blockage but are triggered by the foodstuff that has to do with the ingestion of sugar. Am I correct?

RA: I am Ra. You are partially correct.

QUESTIONER: Then what else causes the spasms?

RA: I am Ra. We speak of two types of cause. The first or proximate cause was a meal with too much oil and too large a burden of undercooked vegetable material. The sugar of the dessert and the few sips of your coffee mixture also were not helpful. The second cause—and this shall be stated clearly—is the energizing of any preexisting condition in order to keep this group from functioning by means of removing the instrument from the ranks of those able to work with those of Ra.

QUESTIONER: Now, there are two areas that the instrument can look to for curing this problem. I understand that the yellow-ray blockage problem has been completely repaired, shall I say. If this is not correct, could you make suggestions on that, please?

RA: I am Ra. Each entity must, in order to completely unblock yellow ray, love all which are in relationship to it, with hope only of the other selves' joy, peace, and comfort.

QUESTIONER: The second thing that the instrument must do to effect this cure is to be careful of diet, which includes all that Ra has just stated and that which Bob recommends from his readings. There seem to be so many different things that can cause this spasm. I was wondering if there were a general approach to food. Could Ra recommend those foods that the instrument could eat that would have no chance of causing a spasm? Could Ra do that?

RA: I am Ra. No.

QUESTIONER: Is that because of the first distortion?

RA: I am Ra. No.

QUESTIONER: Why cannot Ra do that?

RA: I am Ra. There are no foods which this instrument can take with total confidence that no spasm shall occur. The spasming portions of the vehicle have become sensitized through great distortions towards that which you call pain.

QUESTIONER: Is there a group of foods that is most likely to not cause the spasming, or any foods that Ra could name that would be highly likely not to cause spasms?

RA: I am Ra. Yes.

QUESTIONER: Could Ra please state which foods are highly probable to not cause the spasming?

RA: I am Ra. The liquids not containing carbonation, the well-cooked vegetable which is most light and soft, the well-cooked grains, the nonfatted meat such as the fish. You may note that some recommended foodstuffs overlap allergies and sensitivities due to the juvenile rheumatoid arthritic distortions. Further, although sugar such as is in your sweetened desserts represents a potential, we may suggest that it be included at this period for aforementioned reasons.

QUESTIONER: Would Ra please estimate the length of time in our time periods for the probability of this problem, if we follow these curative measures, for this problem to continue with extreme severity?

RA: I am Ra. One of your moon's revolutions has a good possibility/probability vortex of seeing either the worsening of the spastic condition so that surgery becomes indicated, or the bettering of the situation so that the diet continues be watched but the spasms be removed. The housing of the working is within the infection within the duodenum, the stomach, the jejunum, the ileum, the transverse colon, and portions of the liver. This shall be somewhat difficult to remove and constitutes perhaps the most efficient working to date. We may suggest, again, that the one known as Bob may be of aid. The one known as Stuart could, if it wished, discover the infection which is only marginally detectable, but may prefer not to do so. In this case it would be well to request physical aid from an allopathic specialist, such as that which has been mentioned.

QUESTIONER: Do you mean by that Arthur Schoen?

RA: I am Ra. That is correct.

QUESTIONER: You mentioned the possibility of surgery. What would be the surgery to be done, specifically?

RA: I am Ra. The body cannot long bear the extreme acidity which is the environment of such spasms, and will develop the holes or ulcerations which then do appear upon the allopathic testings and suggest to the chirurgeon that which is to be excised.

QUESTIONER: In other words, would this be the removal of a duodenic ulcer that would be performed?

RA: I am Ra. If the ulceration occurs, it shall be past the jejunum and most likely include the ileum and upper portions of the transverse colon.

May we ask for one more query of normal length, as this entity, though filled with enough transferred energy, has the most fragile framework through which we may channel this and our energies.

QUESTIONER: Obviously we would like not to get to the point of surgery. The only other alternative that comes to mind other than the diet and the instrument's mental work is healing through a healer, and I would like Ra's recommendation with respect to a nonallopathic-type healer, and any recommendations that Ra could make for either Jim or myself to act in that capacity or anyone else that Ra could recommend so that we wouldn't have to go through a surgical operation if it seems to become necessary. If we could begin working on one of these other approaches right away, I think it would be highly recommended. Would Ra comment on that, please?

RA: I am Ra. We salute the opening of compassion circuitry in the questioner but note that that which is being experienced by this group is being experienced within an healing atmosphere. The healing hands of each have limited use when the distortion has so many metaphysical layers and mixtures. Therefore, look not to a healing but to the joy of companionship, for each is strong and has its feet set upon the way. The moon casts its shadows. What shall you see? Link hands and walk towards the sun. In this instance this is the greatest healing. For the physical vehicle we can suggest far less than you had hoped.

QUESTIONER: Is there anything that we can do to improve the contact or make the instrument more comfortable?

RA: I am Ra. All is well. Find love and thanksgiving together, and each shall support each. The alignments are conscientious.

We are known to you as Ra. We leave you in the love and in the light of the One Infinite Creator. Go forth, then, merry and glad in His power and peace. Adonai.

Fragment 53

The information in Session 103 concerns the continued spasming condition of Carla's abdominal region. Large amounts of pain accompanied the spasming and caused her to be less and less able to function in any manner of service at all. Thus she felt useless, and her natural joy became reduced and was the focus for this series of questions. Further, Carla had decided to stop buying clothes for a year, because she felt that she had devoted too much time and attention to a transient part of her life and wished to break that habit, and this decision added to her loss of joy.

By June 1983, Don and Luther, our lessor and the owner of the house in which we had lived for all of the Ra sessions, were locked in a Mexican standoff. Because Luther raised the asking price an arbitrary $5,000.00 in the middle of negotiations, and because Don was absolute in his refusal to buy the house without Luther's adhering to his original price, all bets were off. At this point, I was just trying to get Don's deposit out of escrow. Luther would not release it after we agreed not to buy the house. He felt it should be his, regardless. Luther was not a great help. Eventually, I was to agree, long after Don's death, to give him over half the escrow amount. It really didn't seem to matter what was fair. There was more confusion because our lawyer for the purchase of the house did not do his paperwork. I did not want to go to court, feeling that Don would not have done so. Nothing would resolve; everything felt like we were moving in molasses. This was the sort of baffling energy that seemed to have over-taken us. Nothing seemed to work well, me included. Don was feeling poor, too, though in a vague and generalized way rather than anything acute. Jim alone was regaining health every day.

I was concerned about Don without knowing why, really. At this stage of his mental illness, it was very subtle. He simply felt very low and was very prone to think and plan for the worst-case scenario. While he, all his life, was always rigorously careful and cautious in his dealings, a change of address was in order, and his normal response was not this slow. We had to move. But month by month, looking constantly both here and in Atlanta, we could find nothing that Don was pleased with. I would target this point as the time period within which I was becoming aware that something was really wrong. As was always our pattern, I responded to the feelings of concern by asking for help and communicating. Don responded to the same with an increase of reserve. He could be firm about only one thing: that nothing we were looking at was the right place.

In this atmosphere, we were all uneasy, unsettled. I tend to get busy when I get worried. I was busy. All the records were in order. I went on my walks and did my time in the whirlpool and tried to remain hopeful. I felt constantly a bit irritated with Don, because I could never figure out why he rejected every single house we found in the listings or saw from the street. He seemed to be dragging his feet for no reason. Don was never one to share in his motives for doing things. He just said no, much as Nancy Reagan suggested later. It wasn't a solution for either environment. This is the first place I can think back and say, HERE I was feeling both of us losing ground, Don and myself.

I was heavily dependent upon him. I had been raised a most independent person, and I had to learn to let go of everything except what Don needed from me. And Don had needed all my choices to be made around him. He wanted me to be at home and right there, a person he could count on to be loving and willing to do whatever he decided. He never really consulted me, and it sounds very chauvinistic, but he did not mean this personally. He simply consulted no one. He never had. And his view on women was so bad that I could only look better! I quickly formed the opinion that when I stopped getting interference for an idea, that idea was the right one. It took me at least the first six years of our relationship to figure out that no matter what, I should never take a job that took me away from him, even as far as my desk. He even stopped me from working on our projects, many times, when he was at home. "When I am off, you are off," he would say. So I had pretty much given over my decisions to him. It is to be noted that I was aware of the unhealthy tinge of this relationship. However, it was and remains my opinion that this was the absolute best Don could do in the way of having a relationship. And that was good enough for me. Where Don was concerned, I was ready to do whatever he needed. Period.

And at this point, with my health compromised and aiming for more sessions, I was not "allowed" to do much except follow my regimen and try to keep my weight above 80. I was wholeheartedly into this model for living, for what mattered most to me from the first was to see Donald really happy, as only the contact with Ra made him. So our every effort was toward that goal: just to have one more session.

However, what had always before gone hand in hand with my dependency was his willingness to steer our course; indeed, his insistence upon that. I was glad to give this leadership over to him, and to do what he said. He was far wiser than I was or ever could be. When he stopped giving orders and indeed seemed not to know what to do, I was quite lost. My mode was to find out what he wanted, and do it. But with the question of moving, we entered an arena where I could not succeed. No house, no apartment, was acceptable. I do not find it at all odd that I had "lost my joy." I was totally bewildered. My sense of reality had been compromised.

The comments about clothing address a facet of my personality of which I am not proud but do own: I absolutely love to wear a new dress or pair of socks or whatever else might catch my fancy. My childhood had been very low on pretty clothing, as our family finances were tight. My mother and I, when I was grown and her career as a psychologist had begun, had a standing date on Saturday for lunch and shopping, which we kept faithfully until her death in 1991. I would find wonderful things with her, as she was a *champion shopper, looking through great masses of sales racks with the patience of an archaeologist, sifting for good labels and just the right bargain. To this day, when I can, I love to go bargain-hunting and just thrill to be able to wear something new.*

I kept my promise to myself and did not buy clothes for myself for a whole year. However, I cheated, in that I bought things for Momma, and she bought things for me. I kept the letter of the promise anyway!

Session 103 (in total), June 10, 1983

QUESTIONER: The instrument asks the question why she lost her joy in the recent past. Could Ra comment on that?

RA: I am Ra. The instrument made a free-will decision not to address the physical catalyst, causing great pain by means of the allopathically prescribed chemical compound which the instrument was sure would be efficacious due to its reliance upon the suggestions of Ra. Thus the catalyst was given in a more complete form. The outer service to others became nearly impossible, causing the entity to experience once again the choice of the martyr; that is, to put value in a fatal action and die, or to put value on consciousness of the creation of the One Creator and, thereby, live. The instrument, through will, chose the latter path. However, the mind and mental/emotional distortions did not give the support to this decision necessary to maintain the state of unity which this entity nominally experiences and has experienced since its incarnation's beginnings.

Since this catalyst has been accepted, the work begun to remove distortions blocking indigo ray might well be continued apace.

QUESTIONER: Could Ra recommend work appropriate for removing indigo-ray blockage?

RA: I am Ra. We cannot recommend for the general situation, for in each case the distortional vortex is unique. In this particular nexus, the more appropriate working is in the mental and mental/emotional powers of analysis and observation. When the strongest and least distorted complex is set in support, then the less strong portions of the complex shall be strengthened. This entity has long worked with this catalyst. However, this is the first occasion wherein the drugs to dull the pain that sharpens the catalyst have been refused.

QUESTIONER: Can Ra recommend anything that the instrument can do or that we can do to improve any of the energies of the instrument?

RA: I am Ra. This is previously covered material. We have outlined the path the instrument may take in thought.

QUESTIONER: I didn't mean to cover previously covered material. I was hoping to add to this anything that we could do to specifically focus on at this time, the best possible thing that we or the instrument could do to improve these energies, the salient activity.

RA: I am Ra. Before responding, we ask your vigilance during pain flares, as the channel is acceptable but is being distorted periodically by the severe physical distortions of the yellow-ray chemical body of the instrument.

Those salient items for the support group are praise and thanksgiving in harmony. These the group has accomplished with such a degree of acceptability that we cavil not at the harmony of the group. As to the instrument, the journey from worth in action to worth *in esse* is arduous. The entity has denied itself in order to be free of that which it calls addiction. This sort of martyrdom, and here we speak of the small but symbolically great sacrifice of the clothing, causes the entity to frame a selfhood in poorness which feeds unworthiness unless the poverty is seen to be true richness. In other words, good works for the wrong reasons cause confusion and distortion. We encourage the instrument to value itself and to see that its true requirements are valued by the self. We suggest contemplation of true richness of being.

Fragment 54

Ra made a point in Session 104 that seems to us to be one of the central principles that govern our evolution through the third density. It was in reference to the amount of exercise that would be most appropriate for Carla when her body was near normal and when it was weakened by one distortion or another. Ra suggested that it should be exercised more when weakened by distortion because "It is the way of distortion that in order to balance a distortion one must accentuate it."

In the next response, Ra refers to the use of gifts with which one has entered the incarnation as a kind of "Use it or lose it" proposition.

When Book I of *The Law of One* was being published by the Donning Company under the title of *The Ra Material*, we were asked to write an introduction. In one portion of that introduction, Carla was writing about the concept of reincarnation. When we got the galley proofs back from the Donning Company, we noticed that a sentence that we had not written had somehow appeared in what we had written. It was truly "subjectively interesting."

Ra's eloquent closing was in response to a series of queries concerning our oldest cat, Gandalf, who then was going blind and losing weight, apparently in preparation for death. We have considered leaving this material out, once again, because it has little general application, but we have left it in because Ra's desire not to infringe upon our free will is notable and well illustrated here.

When people try to improve their living habits, they always go for diet and exercise as being the first things to change. I think these changes have a mental and emotional benefit as well as a physical one, in that it feels as good for the mind as the body to be doing something when there is a concern. The concern for me, by all three of us, seemed never ending. I don't watch soap operas; they move too slowly for me to keep an interest. But certainly at this point we were living in one. I was steadily losing weight, even eating more than I ever had. So the focus was on diet and exercise. I think we all felt better because we were trying to work on the problems actively. It did, however, seem to take up so much time! Much of the days seemed spent on maintenance. We all were stressed by the situation.

I always have loved my childhood summers spent dancing at the Noyes Rhythm Foundation's camp in Portland, Connecticut. It exists still today and is a wonderful place altogether, one I cannot recommend highly enough, for you can live in a tent, dance on a sprung wood floor to classical piano music in an open pavilion with greenswards and forest about in an absolutely unspoiled environment. The teachers still follow Florence Fleming Noyes's original method of instruction, which posits that all things have their own rhythm, so one may dance a starfish or a star, a bear or a horse, or a blade of grass. It teaches that all things are alive, and that they are all one consciousness. It is very like the Isadora Duncan style of dancing, but with a much-elevated philosophy driving the technique. You can be a beginner and still have a wonderful time. I certainly did, and I measured the exercises I was doing at that time with the yardstick of the dance. (These days the Noyes Rhythm Foundation offers a Senior and a Junior Camp/ School. For more information about this wonderful dance system and the spirits that dance and camp there, write to Shepherd's Nine Summer Creative Arts Center, Noyes School of Rhythm Foundation, 245 Penfield Hill Road, Portland, CT 06480.) The walking came up short! But I was faithful and kept up with the routine. Jim usually was kind enough to walk with me, which motivated me greatly.

I see here, for the first time, really, that Ra was echoing Don's request of me, which always was to take more time just to sit. I am an avid reader and have always loved to toss myself headlong into a romance or science fiction or fantasy novel. To this day it is not unusual for me to read a book a day. Ah, if only the books were "good literature!" —but NO! I love to read just for fun and winkle away to adventure land. As time has passed, I have more and more found the time to rest in silence but still tend to read too much.

The stomach problems were to plague me for some years; indeed, still. But things were greatly aided in 1988, when my doctor finally figured out that my gall bladder was infected. Ever since 1982, they had been reading the picture of my gall bladder as showing some sludge—not an operable problem. However, in actuality it was simply infected, and not working at all. Until the sick organ was removed, I was to suffer greatly. And four years later, in 1992, I had the second cleansing operation, when half my colon was removed. These days, I still deal with discomfort throughout the GI tract, but it is not beyond management, and most days I can do well and just put such aches and pains out of my mind. When the sessions were going on in 1983, however, I was in sorry shape. The stress of knowing things weren't right with Don was undoubtedly a factor here.

One can note the way Ra moved fluidly between the psyche and the soma in working with illness. They linked the severity of the pain to work in consciousness, which I was pursuing as intensively as I could, but to slow avail. When one has felt unworthy for a long time, one is slow to learn self-respect of the deep and lasting kind. I was embarking on a life lesson, which was all about learning to be wise and live. Don was also embarking upon a journey, a much-darker one. He was learning how to love completely and die.

Meanwhile our beloved cat, Gandalf, was getting old and creaky. How he loved us! He wanted only to be on us, or beside us, always. His devotion never let up, even when, in Georgia some months later, we had to lift him to the food and sandbox, as he could no longer walk. He would move heaven and earth just to be with us, and I got in the habit of carrying him with me so he would not have to walk on his sore paws.

It may seem like Donald spent a lot of time on this kitty, but you have to remember how much like a child such a special pet is. We had no children; being celibate, he wasn't likely to sire a family. But we did have Gandalf and Fairchild. They meant a great deal to us, as our cats still do to Jim and me.

Notice how the tuning started drifting as Don persisted in trying to get specific information from Ra. It is abuse of a well-tuned channel to ask for specific information, I think. And notice how Ra's suggestions for bettering a situation always begin with rejoicing in, giving thanks for and praising the situation, whatever it is. To Ra's way of thinking, when the attitude with which you met the moment was praise and thanksgiving, you'd be best prepared to meet it well. Simple advice, hard to follow, but worth it.

Session 104 (in total), July 27, 1983

RA: I am Ra. We greet you in the love and in the light of the One Infinite Creator. We communicate now.

QUESTIONER: Could you first please give me the condition of the instrument?

RA: I am Ra. The readings are somewhat less distorted towards physical bankruptcy and vital-energy loss than at the previous asking. There is still considerable bias in these readings.

QUESTIONER: The instrument would like to know what is the optimum amount of aerobics, walking, and whirlpool exercises for the best condition at this time.

RA: I am Ra. We shall answer in two ways. Firstly, to speak to the general case which pertains to this instrument in varying degree. Each form of exercise is well accomplished approximately three to four times per your week. The amount of exercise, all quantified as one sum, is approximately one hour per diurnal period.
    We now answer in a second way, distorted in this response to the duple conditions of yellow-ray, physical difficulty and mind complex distortion. The swirling waters then must needs be viewed as being appropriate four to five of your times per week. The walking and the exercising as much as is desired by the entity. The total of all these should in no case exceed ninety minutes per diurnal period.
    The yellow-ray, physical body has been experiencing that which is called lupoid changes in much tissue of muscle and some of the organs as well.
    The exercise regains the wasting physical muscular strength. In some ways the walking is the more appropriate exercise due to the proximity of the entity to second-density creatures, particularly your trees. However, the habitation you enjoy does not offer such opportunity and instead offers the proximity to creations of mind/body/spirit complexes. This does not feed the mental/emotional needs of this entity, although it produces the same physical result. The exercise fulfills more of the mental/emotional need due to the entity's fondness

for rhythmic expressions of the body, such as those found in athletic endeavors derivative of the artifact system which is known among your peoples as the dance.

We suggest the support group encourage any exercise except that which exceeds the time limit, which is already far beyond the physical limitations of this body complex. It is the way of distortion that in order to balance a distortion one must accentuate it. Thusly, the over-wearing of the body may, if correctly motivated, produce a lack of deficit at which juncture the lesser exercise limitations should be put into practice.

QUESTIONER: The instrument has determined that the unwise use of her will is its use without the joy and faith components and constitutes martyrdom. Would Ra comment on that, please?

RA: I am Ra. We are pleased that the entity has pondered that which has been given. We would comment as follows. It is salubrious for the instrument to have knowledge which is less distorted towards martyrdom and which is rich in promise. The entity which is strong to think shall either be strong to act or that which it has shall be removed. Thus manifestation of knowledge is an area to be examined by the instrument.

We would further note that balancing, which in this entity's case is best accomplished in analysis and manifestation seated with the contemplation of silence, may be strengthened by manifested silence and lack of routine activity. We may go no further than this recommendation of regularized leisure, and desire that the entity discover the fundamental truths of these distortions as it will.

QUESTIONER: Is there anything further that we can do to help the instrument's stomach and back-spasming problem?

RA: I am Ra. The greatest aid is already being given to the fullest. The encouragement of the instrument to refrain from the oil-fried nature of foodstuffs in its intake is helpful. Cheerful harmony is helpful. The spasms must subside as a function of the entity's indigo-ray work and, to some extent, the recommendations made in response to a previous query. The definitive refraining from over-stepping the already swollen boundaries of physical limitation is recommended. The infection remains and the symptoms are now far less medicable, the entity having chosen the catalyst.

QUESTIONER: Can you tell us what is wrong with our cat's, Gandalf's eyes?

RA: I am Ra. The one known as Gandalf nears the end of its incarnation. Its eyesight dims and the aqueous membrane becomes tough. This is not a comfortable circumstance but is one which causes the entity no true discomfort.

QUESTIONER: Is there anything that we can do to alleviate this situation?

RA: I am Ra. There is a course of therapy which would aid the situation. However, we do not recommend it as the condition is more benign than the treatment.

QUESTIONER: I don't understand. Could you explain what you meant?

RA: I am Ra. A doctor of the allopathic tradition would give you the drops for the eyes. The cat would find the experience of being confined while the drops were given more distorted than the discomfort it now feels but is able to largely ignore.

QUESTIONER: Can the cat see at all?

RA: I am Ra. Yes.

QUESTIONER: Does it seem that the cat will lose all of its vision in the very near future, or is the cat very near death?

RA: I am Ra. The one known as Gandalf will not lose eyesight or life on most possibility/probability vortices for three of your seasons, approximately.

QUESTIONER: I feel very bad about the condition of the cat and really would like to help it. Can Ra suggest anything that we can do to help out Gandalf?

RA: I am Ra. Yes.

QUESTIONER: What would that be?

RA: I am Ra. Firstly, we would suggest that possibility/probability vortices include those in which the entity known as Gandalf has a lengthier incarnation. Secondly, we would suggest that this entity goes to a graduation if it desires. Otherwise, it may choose to reincarnate to be with those companions it has loved. Thirdly, the entity known to you as

Betty has the means of making the entity more distorted towards comfort/discomfort.

QUESTIONER: Could you tell me who you mean by Betty? I'm not sure that I know who you mean by Betty. And what Betty would do?

RA: I am Ra. The one known as Carla has this information.

QUESTIONER: I'm concerned about the possibility of moving. If we did move, it would make it very difficult for Gandalf to find his way around a new place if he can't see. Does he see enough to be able to find his way around a new environment?

RA: I am Ra. The vision is less than adequate but is nearly accommodated by a keen sense of smell and of hearing. The companions and the furnishings being familiar, a new milieu would be reasonably expected to be satisfactorily acceptable within a short period of your space/time.

QUESTIONER: Could we administer the drops that you spoke of that would help his eyesight so that he wouldn't be confined? Is there any way that we could do that?

RA: I am Ra. It is unlikely.

QUESTIONER: There's nothing that we can do? Is there any other possibility of using any techniques to help his eyesight?

RA: I am Ra. No.

QUESTIONER: Is this loss of eyesight . . . What is the metaphysical reason for the loss of eyesight? What brought it about?

RA: I am Ra. In this case the metaphysical component is tiny. This is the condign catalyst of old age.

QUESTIONER: Would the drops that you spoke of that would aid the eyesight . . . How much would they aid the eyesight if they were administered?

RA: I am Ra. Over a period of applications the eyesight would improve somewhat, perhaps 20, perhaps 30 percent. The eye region would feel less tight. Balanced against this is rapidly increasing stiffness of motion so that the holding in a still position is necessarily quite uncomfortable.

QUESTIONER: Then Ra thinks that the benefit derived from these drops would not be worth the cat's discomfort. This would probably … Is there any way that the cat could be given anesthetic and the drops put into the eyes so that the cat was not aware of them?

RA: I am Ra. The harm done by putting the allopathic anesthetic into the body complex of this harvestable entity far overshadows the stillness accruing therefrom which would allow administration of medicaments.

QUESTIONER: I'm sorry to belabor this subject so much, but I was really hoping to come up with something to help Gandalf. I assume then that Ra has suggested that we leave things as they are. How many applications of drops would be necessary to get some help for the eyes, roughly?

RA: Approximately forty to sixty.

QUESTIONER: Each day, or something like that?

RA: I am Ra. Please expel breath over this instrument's breast. [This was done as directed.]

QUESTIONER: Is that satisfactory?

RA: I am Ra. Yes.

QUESTIONER: I had asked if the drops should be administered once per diurnal period. Is that correct?

RA: I am Ra. This depends upon the allopathic physician from whom you receive them.

QUESTIONER: What is the name of the drops?

RA: I am Ra. We have a difficulty. Therefore, we shall refrain from answering this query.

QUESTIONER: I am sorry to belabor this point. I am very concerned about the cat, and I understand that Ra recommends that we do not use the drops and we won't. I just wanted to know what it was that we weren't doing that would help the eyesight, and I apologize for belaboring this point. I'll close just by asking Ra if there is any further recommendation that he could make with respect to this cat.

RA: I am Ra. Rejoice in its companionship.

QUESTIONER: When we got our introduction back from our publisher on the book which originally was called *The Law of One*, in the introduction Carla had been speaking on reincarnation, and there was this sentence added: "For although originally part of Jesus' teachings they were censored from all subsequent editions by the Empress." Would Ra please comment on the source of that being placed in our introduction?

RA: I am Ra. This follows the way of subjectively interesting happenings, conditions, circumstances, or coincidences.
We would suggest one more full query at this time.

QUESTIONER: Prior to the veiling process there was, I am assuming, no archetypical plan for the evolutionary process. It was totally left up to the free will of the mind/body/spirits to evolve in any way that they desired. Is this correct?

RA: I am Ra. No.
I am Ra. We leave you in appreciation of the circumstances of the great illusion in which you now choose to play the pipe and timbrel and move in rhythm. We are also players upon a stage. The stage changes. The acts ring down. The lights come up once again. And throughout the grand illusion and the following and the following, there is the undergirding majesty of the One Infinite Creator. All is well. Nothing is lost. Go forth rejoicing in the love and the light, the peace, and the power of the One Infinite Creator. I am Ra. Adonai.

Fragment 55
After a good deal of searching, we finally did find a house north of Atlanta to which we were about to move in November 1983. We decided to query Ra about the metaphysical cleansing needs of this new dwelling before moving there, and that was the purpose of this session. As Jim was giving Carla her presession massage, he noted reddened welts, symmetrical in nature, on both sides of her back. They were similar to the welting that had covered her body when her kidneys failed at age thirteen from glomerulo nephritis. Apparently,

if Carla had chosen to meet difficulties in completing our lease agreement with our landlord by allowing a feeling of separation from him to occur or had allowed this same feeling of separation to grow for Don as he hemmed and hawed about what house to choose in Atlanta, that allowing of separation of self from other-self could have been energized by our negative friend until her self was separated from her physical vehicle, and her incarnation would have been at its end. She had to deal with our landlord, who had numerous requirements for our leaving that he felt justified in making, and with Don's mental condition, which was beginning to show further signs of the long-term stress to mind and body that commuting and worrying about his job had brought about. Strikes and bankruptcy were continually threatening Eastern Airlines, and, though he knew it would be easier to get to work from his base in Atlanta, he had great difficulty in even looking at houses in Atlanta, much less choosing one, because of his lifelong love of Louisville and the comfort and beauty of our home as we had known it together. But our home was up for sale, and we had to move somewhere.

My first trip with the 24-foot U-Haul truck saw me lost in the mountains of northern Georgia. Many curves and turns later, I found our new home in the countryside around Lake Lanier. It was midnight when I saw the house for the first time—Don and Carla had picked it out—and I immediately began searching in the darkness for each window and doorway to perform the ritual of cleansing with salt and blessed water. It was an inauspicious beginning to an unusual experience there.

A small beginning is made near the end of this session to query again on the archetypical mind, and Ra's comment at the end of this session is a key part of the mystery of Don's illness and his death.

By the time Don accepted the house we moved into, he was in a settled state of disorientation, something unknown before this time. I, too, was quite at low ebb. Dimly grasping that I needed to be exquisitely correct in all ethical dealings, and willing to go to almost any lengths to remain in the light, I did manage to keep the anger and vast irritation I felt with our landlord out of my actual dealings with him. We packed up the kitties and Don flew us down to Atlanta. Friends drove our cars down, another friend drove the second rental van, and we piled into a huge and glamorous—and decidedly nonwinterized—lakefront house in Cumming, Georgia. As if warning us that this trip was going to be dicey, Jim's first attempt to take the van to Georgia found him fetched up, barely 60 miles from Louisville, with a broken truck. We disregarded this event and pressed on.

The whole five months that we were there was like a sitcom, overlaid with bizarre situations. Cumming was the county seat of Forsythe County, a place notorious for its prejudice against any race but Caucasian. On a Saturday, one could drive through the little town and see Ku Klux Klan members in regalia, except for their head masks and hats, handing out brochures at the stop lights. Grandmothers, children, all ages, and both sexes wore these sad little costumes and waved racial hatred around as though it were cotton candy. I had planned to join the Robert Shaw Chorale, but when I sang my piece, there was a misunderstanding, and the judges thought I had sung a wrong note. So I did not get accepted, something I had not even thought of. I had been singing all my life, and I was a competent chorus member. But I was out. Instead, needing to sing, I found a little group in the Cumming area and plodded along while I was there with Irish folk songs and the like, fun to sing but not the marvelous prayer experience I had always found classical sacred choral singing to offer. I planned to sing, on Sundays, at the cathedral there, St. Philip's, and had made every arrangement to do so. But they would not let me start singing until after Christmas, a practice the church had been forced to adopt after people tried to drop in for Christmas and not sing the rest of the year. Meanwhile, I found a mission church five minutes from our house, which had no choir whatever. So I stayed in tiny All Saints' mission and sang the old Anglican hymns during Eucharist. Every expectation was baffled. Nothing worked out as envisioned.

The worst of it was that Don had more, not less, to do in order to arrive at work. He had to run the whole gamut of paralyzing traffic from far north of Atlanta to south of it, where the airport was. And the weather seemed fated to make things harder. It was extremely cold in Georgia that winter, and when icing conditions were there, as was the case several times, there was absolutely no way to drive anywhere. I can remember Don having to stay in a motel he managed to slide into the parking lot of, unable to reach either home or work. Christmas Eve found me singing two services at All Saints' while Jim and Don bailed water from burst pipes. By the time the New Year came, the wet carpets had begun to become moldy, and both Don and I were allergic to mold and mildew. As luxurious as the house was for fun on the lake in summer, it was nothing short of a disaster as far as winter living went. I got ulcers on my toes because they were so cold—the floor was never warmer than 50 degrees, ever.

Since all this was wrong with the house, we immediately began looking again for another house, both in Atlanta and back in Louisville. We never had one settled day in Georgia, and, pretty as the state was, I cannot say I would wish to be there again. Until Don found the house we now live in, in March, we were in a constant restless perch, having no real order to things. Our belongings remained boxed, our feelings fragile. I was the one who dealt with the new landlord, which was not a picnic. Don was very insistent that we move immediately for the whole time there, so even though we did stay in that one place for five months, the landlord and I had to talk at least weekly so that he could be apprised of our latest plans—none of which worked out. Finally, in March, he asked us to leave, so that his family could use the house themselves that summer. It was at that juncture that Don flew to Louisville by himself over a weekend, found this lovely and venerable old bungalow in which we still live, and agreed to buy it.

Buying a house was something Don had always felt was unwise for himself to do. And as soon as he had done it, he began to regret it. For Jim and me, this was most difficult to bear, as we had unwisely let ourselves hope that we would come to this little exurb and really settle in and just live as we had before. But Don remained convinced that we must move, again, while always turning down any possible place we found to look at. When I found a house twenty thousand dollars cheaper, with a duplex design that would give Don and me a full home plus an apartment for Jim, and Don turned that down too, I realized that something was really wrong. Things were in a fine pickle.

In this atmosphere, it was faintly off-balance even to try to pursue the work and questioning about the archetypical mind that we had begun, but persist we did, cleansing the new working room daily and hoping for the day when we could have another session with those of Ra. I remember feelings of great hope and faith welling up within me as this period spent itself, and wonderings about what in the world was happening with Don. None of us knew anything to do except persevere, and follow Ra's suggestion to meet all with praise and thanks. Or try!

Session 105 (in total), October 19, 1983

RA: I am Ra. I greet you, my friends, in the love and in the light of the One Infinite Creator. We communicate now.

QUESTIONER: Could you first please give me the condition of the instrument?

RA: I am Ra. The vital energies of this instrument are in a much more biased state than the previous asking, with the faculties of will and faith having regained their prominent place in this entity's existence and balance. The physical deficit continues.

QUESTIONER: I am sorry that we have to ask so many maintenance questions. We seem to be in a confused condition now with respect to our abilities to continue in the direction that we wish to with respect to the archetypical mind.

I would like to ask what caused the symmetrical welts on the instrument's back, and is there anything further that we can do to heal the instrument and her condition, including these welts?

RA: I am Ra. The welting is a symptom of that which has been a prolonged psychic greeting. The opportunity for this entity to experience massive allergic reaction from streptococcal and staphylococcal viruses has been offered in hopes that this entity would wish to leave the incarnation. The previous occurrence of this state of the mind complex, which occurred upon, in your time-numbering system, the ninth month, the twelfth day, of your present planetary solar revolution, caught your fifth-density companion unprepared. The entity is now prepared.

There have been two instances wherein this entity could have started the reaction since the first opportunity was missed. Firstly, the opportunity to separate self from other-self in connection with the choosing of a house. Secondly, the possible vision of self separated from other-self in regard to the dissolving of mundane bonds concerning the leaving of this dwelling. Both opportunities were met by this entity with a refusal to separate self from other-self, with further work also upon the indigo-ray level concerning the avoidance of martyrdom while maintaining unity in love.

Thusly, this instrument has had its immunal defenses breached and its lymphatic system involved in the invasion of these viri. You may see some merit in a purging of the instrument's yellow-ray, chemical body in order to more quickly aid the weakened body complex in its attempt to remove these substances. Techniques include therapeutic enemas or colonics, the sauna once or twice in a day, and the use of vigorous rubbing of the integument for the period of approximately seven of your diurnal periods.

We speak not of diet, not because it might not aid but because this entity ingests small quantities of any substance and is already avoiding certain substances, notably fresh milk and oil.

QUESTIONER: Is there any particular place that the integument should be vigorously rubbed?

RA: I am Ra. No.

QUESTIONER: Could you please tell me what caused Jim's kidney problem to return, and what can be done to heal it?

RA: I am Ra. The entity, Jim, determined that it would cleanse itself and thus would spend time/space and space/time in pursuit and contemplation of perfection. The dedication to this working was intensified until the mind/body/spirit complex rang in harmony with this intention. The entity did not grasp the literal way in which metaphysical intentions are translated by the body complex of one working in utter unity of purpose. The entity began the period of prayer, fasting, penitence, and rejoicing. The body complex, which was not yet fully recovered from the nephrotic syndrome, began to systematically cleanse each organ, sending all the detritus that was not perfect through kidneys which were not given enough liquid to dilute the toxins being released. The toxins stayed with the body complex and reactivated a purely physical illness. There is no metaphysical portion in this relapse.

The healing is taking place in manifestation of an affirmation of body complex health, which, barring untoward circumstance, shall be completely efficacious.

QUESTIONER: Is any consideration of the appropriateness of the house at Lake Lanier which we intend to move to or special preparation other than that planned advisable?

RA: I am Ra. We believe you have queried obliquely. Please requery.

QUESTIONER: We plan to cleanse the property at the Lake Lanier location, using the techniques prescribed by Ra having to do with using the salt for thirty-six hours, etc. I would like to know if this is sufficient or if there is any salient problem with respect to moving to that house that Ra could advise upon at this time, please.

RA: I am Ra. The cleansing of the dwelling of which you speak need be only three nights and two days. This dwelling is benign. The techniques are acceptable. We find three areas in which use of garlic as previously described would be beneficial. Firstly, the bunk-bed room, below the top sleeping pallet. Secondly, the exterior of the dwelling facing the road and centering about the small rocks approximately two-thirds of the length of the dwelling from the driveway side.

Thirdly, there is the matter of the boathouse. We suggest weekly cleansings of that area with garlic, the cut onions, and the walking of a light-filled perimeter. The garlic and onion, renewed weekly, should remain permanently hung, suspended from string or wire between workings.

QUESTIONER: Just so that I don't make a mistake in interpreting your directions with respect to the second area outside the house, could you give me a distance and magnetic compass heading from the exact center of the dwelling to that position?

RA: I am Ra. We may only be approximate but would suggest a distance of 37 feet, a magnetic heading of 84 to 92 degrees.

QUESTIONER: I know that it is unimportant for our purposes, and from the philosophical point of view I don't want to do anything to upset the Law of Confusion, so don't feel that it is necessary to answer this, but I was wondering what condition created the necessity for such continual cleansing of the boathouse?

RA: I am Ra. The intent is to create a perimeter within which the apiary denizens will not find it necessary to sting and indeed will not find it promising to inhabit.

QUESTIONER: Are you speaking of bees or wasps or creatures of that type?

RA: I am Ra. That is so.

QUESTIONER: Are Jim's plans and ritual for the deconsecrating of this dwelling sufficient, or should something be added or changed?

RA: I am Ra. No change is necessary. The points necessary to be included in consecration or deconsecration of the place are covered. We may suggest that each second-density, woody plant which you have invested during your tenancy within this dwelling be thanked and blessed.

QUESTIONER: Is there any other suggestion that Ra could make with respect to any part of this move that is planned, and will it—will we have any problems at all in contacting Ra in the new dwelling, and if so, will Ra tell us about those and what we could do to alleviate any problems in contacting Ra in the new dwelling?

RA: I am Ra. We weigh this answer carefully, for it comes close to abrogation of free will, but find the proximity acceptable due to this instrument's determination to be of service to the One Infinite Creator regardless of personal circumstances.

Any physical aid upon the part of the instrument in the packing and unpacking will activate those allergic reactions lying dormant for the most part at this time. This entity is allergic to those items which are unavoidable in transitions within your third-density illusion; that is, dust, mildew, etc. The one known as Bob will be of aid in this regard. The scribe should take care also to imbibe a doubled quantity of liquids in order that any allergically caused toxins may be flushed from the body complex.

There is no difficulty in resuming contact through this tuned instrument with the social memory complex, Ra, in the chosen dwelling, or, indeed, in any place whatsoever once physical and metaphysical cleansing has been accomplished.

QUESTIONER: I have come to the conclusion that the meaning of the hawk that we had about a year ago when we started to move the first time had to do with the nonbenign nature of the house, in the metaphysical sense, which I had picked. If it would not interfere with the Law of Confusion, I think that it would be philosophically interesting to know if I am correct with respect to that.

RA: I am Ra. What bird comes to affirm for Ra? What bird would be chosen to warn? We ask the questioner to ponder these queries.

QUESTIONER: We have been, you might say, experimentally determining a lot of things about the body, the next portion of the tarot, and have been experiencing some of the feedback effects, you might say, between the mind and the body. From everything that we have done so far with respect to these effects, the great value of the third-density, yellow-ray body at this time is as a device that feeds back catalyst to create the polarization, I would say. I would ask Ra if initially, when they were designed for third-density experience, the mind/body/spirits—not the mind/body/spirit complexes—had as the major use of the yellow-ray body the feeding back of catalyst, and if not, what was the purpose of the yellow-ray body?

RA: I am Ra. The description which began your query is suitable for the function of the mind/body/spirit or the mind/body/spirit complex. The position in creation of physical manifestation changed not one whit when the veil of forgetting was dropped.

QUESTIONER: Then the yellow-ray body, from the very beginning, was designed as what Ra has called an athanor for the mind, a device to accelerate the evolution of the mind. Is this correct?

RA: I am Ra. It is perhaps more accurate to note that the yellow-ray, physical vehicle is a necessity, without which the mind/body/spirit complex cannot pursue evolution at any pace.

QUESTIONER: Then you are saying that the evolution of that portion of the individual that is not yellow ray is not possible without the clothing at intervals in the yellow-ray body. Is this correct?

RA: I am Ra. No.

QUESTIONER: Would you clear up my thinking on that? I didn't quite understand your statement.

RA: I am Ra. Each mind/body/spirit or mind/body/spirit complex has an existence simultaneous with that of creation. It is not dependent upon any physical vehicle. However, in order to evolve, change, learn, and manifest the Creator, the physical vehicles appropriate to each density are necessary. Your query implied that physical vehicles accelerated growth. The more accurate description is that they permit growth.

QUESTIONER: As an example I would like to take the distortion of a disease or bodily malfunction prior to the veil and compare it to that after the veil. Let us assume that the conditions that Jim experienced with respect to his kidney malfunction had been an experience that occurred prior to the veil. Would this experience have occurred prior to the veil? Would it have been different? And if so, how?

RA: I am Ra. The anger of separation is impossible without the veil. The lack of awareness of the body's need for liquid is unlikely without the veil. The decision to contemplate perfection in discipline is quite improbable without the veil.

QUESTIONER: I would like to examine a sample, shall we say, bodily distortion prior to the veil and how it would affect the mind. Could Ra give an example of that, please?

RA: I am Ra. This general area has been covered. We shall recapitulate here.
    The patterns of illness, diseases, and death are a benignant demesne[5] within the plan of incarnational experience. As such, some healing would occur by decision of mind/body/spirits, and incarnations were experienced with the normal ending of illness to death, accepted

as such since without the veil it is clear that the mind/body/spirit continues. Thusly, the experiences, both good and bad, or joyful and sad, of the mind/body/spirit before veiling would be pale, without vibrancy or the keen edge of interest that such brings in the postveiling mind/body/spirit complex.

QUESTIONER: At the end of an incarnation, before veiling, did the entity appear physically to have aged like entities at the end of their incarnation in our present illusion? Did the Significator look like that?

RA: I am Ra. The Significator of Mind, Body, or Spirit is a portion of the archetypical mind and looks as each envisions such to appear. The body of mind/body/spirits before veiling showed all the signs of aging which acquaint you now with the process leading to the removal from third-density incarnation of the mind/body/spirit complex. It is well to recall that the difference betwixt mind/body/spirits and mind/body/spirit complexes is a forgetting within the deeper mind. Physical appearances and surface and instinctual activities are much the same.

QUESTIONER: Then I was wondering what was the root reason for the change in appearance that we see as the aging process. I am trying to uncover the basic philosophical premise here, but I may be shooting in the dark and not questioning on it correctly. I am trying to get at the reason behind the design in this change in appearance, when it seems to me that it would be just as possible for the mind/body/spirit or mind/body/spirit complex to look the same throughout an incarnation. Could Ra explain the reason for this change?

RA: I am Ra. When the discipline of the personality has led the mind/body/spirit complex into the fifth and especially the sixth level of study, it is no longer necessary to build destruction of the physical vehicle into its design, for the spirit complex is so experienced as a shuttle that it is aware when the appropriate degree of intensity of learning and increment of lesson have been achieved. Within third density, not to build into the physical vehicle its ending would be counterproductive to the mind/body/spirit complexes therein residing, for within the illusion it seems more lovely to be within the illusion than to drop the garment which has carried the mind/body/spirit complex and move on.

QUESTIONER: I see, then, that it is, shall we say, when an individual reaches a very old age it becomes apparent to him in third density that he is worn out. Therefore, be is not attached to this vehicle as firmly as he would be with a good-looking, well-functioning one.

After the veil, the body is definitely an athanor for the mind. Prior to the veiling, did the body serve as an athanor for the mind at all?

RA: I am Ra. Yes.

You may ask one more full query.

QUESTIONER: I believe that I should ask if there is anything that we can do to make the instrument more comfortable or to improve the contact, since in the last session I was not able to get that question in.

RA: I am Ra. We find the weariness of the group well balanced by its harmony. That weariness shall continue in any future circumstance during your incarnations. Therefore, look you to your love and thanksgiving for each other and join always in fellowship, correcting each broken strand of that affection with patience, comfort, and quietness. We find all meticulously observed in the alignments and give you these words only as reminder. All that can be done for the instrument seems done with an whole heart, and the instrument itself is working in the indigo ray with perseverance.

We have previously mentioned some temporary measures for the instrument. If these are adopted, additional liquids shall be imbibed by the instrument and by the questioner, whose bond with the instrument is such that each difficulty for one is the same in sympathy for the other.

I am Ra. I leave you rejoicing merrily in the love and the light, the power, and the peace of the One Infinite Creator. Adonai.

Fragment 56

We lived in the house on Lake Lanier for five months—from November 1983 until April 1984—before deciding that that experiment had been a failure. We were able to have only one session with Ra during that time because Don's physical condition was worsening, and his worry was increasing his mental distortions as well. Most of the time, Carla's physical condition was also below the level necessary to safely attempt contact with Ra. In January 1984, Don's condition became so bad that he was forced to call in sick for the first time in his nineteen years with Eastern Airlines. He would fly only a few more trips before his death that November.

However, as we were about to move back to Louisville, Don was able to gin himself up to be in good-enough condition for a Ra session, so we could ask about the metaphysical cleansing needs of our new home as well as ask about Don's and Carla's difficulties. Ra's reference to Carla's "inappropriate use of compassion" concerns her response to Don's continued worrying about his job, his health, and the continuance of our work. One afternoon while, Don was sharing his worries, Carla simply told him that she would take over those worries for him, and he could do what she usually did: relax, have a good time, and be carefree. Don innocently agreed. The bond of unity between Don and Carla was apparently of such a nature that this simple agreement resulted in a deleterious transfer of energy between them. This occurred at a time when both were apparently under-going an internal process of transformation that is usually called initiation.

We can assume that our friend of negative fifth density found targets of opportunities within these combined experiences of initiation and the negative energy transfer and was able to increase their intensity. The mystery-filled nature of the cumulative situation becomes more evident here, as we do not know why Carla survived and Don didn't. We can only remind ourselves of Ra's parting words after this last session, when Ra suggested, "the nature of all manifestation to be illusory and functional only insofar as the entity turns from shape and shadow to the One."

At the time of this session, I had gone through every kind of alarm and concern you could possibly imagine. Don had stopped eating, more or less. He was acting extremely unlike himself, and while I had not yet realized he was psychotic and not entirely in our usual reality, I was disturbed and scared by these changes. Don's entire pattern of previous behavior had trained me to respond to his wishes. Don picked our meal times, our movie dates; he liked and received total control over my life. Call me dependent and you'd be right. However, it was the only way Don could bear the intimacy of a live-in relationship. I could object and be heard; I could suggest and sometimes get lucky, but on the whole, Don was an old-fashioned man who liked me to be at home, period. I awaited his fancy. Meanwhile, I read or did quiet desk work.

Suddenly, he was always asking me what I had to do next, and then driving me, a chore that hurt his piles and that he usually left to Jim (I was at that point no longer driving; it hurt too much). He simply sat while I went to church, to exercise class, to the folksong rehearsals. Even though Jim was swamped with things to do for L/L business, for the landlord, who had him dig a root cellar out of red-orange clay, and for the house, Don began to try hard to stay in and eat at home every night, also a radical departure from his usual wont. Jim was off-balance—I think that's as far as his humor was affected. He was puzzled. But I was in full nervous collapse.

I feel that B.C. and I really did merge into one mind, one person, in that "inappropriate" transfer between us, triggered by my suggestion to switch roles, and his agreement. Between us, we had a simple dynamic: he was wise and I was loving. Actually, we shared much ground, but our deeper natures were quite polarized between wisdom and love. In that transfer, Don received the extreme sensitivity with which I receive all sense impression, and the fully expressing and open nature of my heart. And I received in full strength the stark terror that lived behind Don's calm and oh-so-blue eyes, tempered by his firm and very solid grasp on the big picture.

I have come to feel that in the time from this session, which was done two weeks before we left Atlanta, thankfully to return to the blessed hills of Kentucky, until B.C.'s death in November of that year, Don was able to complete an entire incarnational course of how to open his heart. I cannot express how much agony and suffering he sustained in this time. The concrete walls that were so very strong and had protected him always, fell away as if they were never there, and he felt everything. And how he loved! He could not watch television, even the sitcoms, because there was too much suffering. He, the lifelong observer by actual oath, cried at the Mary Tyler Moore Show. And when he was in the same room with me, he tried, over and over, to explain to me just how bad the situation was. This one thought was uppermost in his mind, always. The sheer horror of what he was feeling wiped him fairly clean of most other emotion, and he was unable to remain collected for long around me.

Meanwhile, I was utterly and damnably unaware of Don's fears that I preferred Jim. When Don began snatching me to him and kissing me, not knowing his strength, he hurt me, cracked a rib, split the skin of my lips against my teeth, left bruises, even, when he was in hospital in May, put me into the hospital with him, with sciatic nerve pain, which I'd gotten having to stay in an uncomfortable chair for several hours (to Don, this was the only chair that was not bugged). I became frightened of Don. I began waking up in the morning to find Don sitting beside me, waiting patiently for me to awaken. When he had said, "Good morning," he simply began telling me how bad everything was. No matter how I attempted to get him to relax, take it easy, do what the professionals had said about exercise and medication, and trust in time to heal—all of which I tried to retail to him, with absolutely no success, he was utterly sure nothing could get better, ever. For him, reality really began to slip away, to the point where I was afraid to ride with him. My nerves broke under this most difficult strain. I was completely downcast, for I could not find Don, and all I could think was that I didn't have him to go to—I had to keep together by myself on behalf of me AND L/L Research, because Don was no longer with us. He seemed a different person altogether. The color of his eyes even changed from deep, brilliant sky blue to navy. I'd been doing his paperwork for a long time. I knew that Don had slightly more than two years of built-up sick time with the airlines, and had interacted with everyone who had to be notified of his illness. Everyone, to a man, wanted nothing more than that Don take all that time, if that's what it took, to get it together again. The crises in his head were not real to me, or to Jim. Only he had the awful sense of impending economic doom. Don made a comfortable salary. His expenses for all three of us and the kitties cost him about half his check, usually, each month. But Don lost all hope, and truly that being that he became was living in hell.

And how can I look at that and say that it is all part of a perfect pattern? Only by having been given the grace to see it, finally, after many years of gazing at the riveting scenes in memory, probing them and working with them over the days, months, and years since Don died. Fifteen years have passed, and that gives a much-clearer perspective. In accepting at last the importance of the open and giving heart to balance wisdom, Don completed the personal lesson he intended to learn. Opening his heart killed his body, but truly he was rejoicing not a day after he was gone from the physical illusion, for he appeared to me several times joyful and laughing and telling me all was well. And I, my nerves permanently less than they were before the Ra contact and Don's death, have embarked upon that balancing of the compassion I have been given and earned in this next lesson, which began the day Don died.

When I woke the morning after Don's suicide, I expected my hair to be completely white. There was no outer change. But I began a completely new life at this point. Until November 1990, I spent my time in self-judgment almost entirely. I had found out about Don's suspicions of me and felt that he had enlarged these fears until he'd killed himself over them. It was my fault, not because I was guilty of any sort of infidelity, but because I should have guessed what he was thinking, and reassured him. But this never occurred to me, in my foolish pride. I just assumed that he would KNOW that I, that paragon of virtue, would never break an agreement. I really have a continuing problem with pride, because I do try to be exact in my ethics. I got completely blindsided with Don's illness.

It was further confusing that every doctor, social worker, and friend suggested the same thing—that Jim and I needed to let him alone, not to try to bribe him to do things, because he was going to have to make the decision to get well himself, and we would only lengthen the process if we fussed. Looking back, how I wish I had had the vision to say "NUTS" to that and just stay with him no matter what. And yet, as I tried my best to do just that, vowing to stay if it killed me, my body simply went dumb on me, and I woke up one morning pretty out of touch with reality. From March onward, my beloved Don was in full and fast decline, and I was walking through a complete nervous breakdown.

The allergies that had Don so worried about the Hobbs Park house were on his mind because of the lake house's unhappy brush with being flooded by burst pipes that frigid Christmas Eve. The damp had penetrated deep into the thick wall-to-wall carpeting in the hallway and rendered about half the house unlivable for me and Don. When we arrived here, we found a dry basement, or rather a basement with a sump pump and no unusual drainage problems. The humidity was fine, and the place was, indeed, a very angelic-feeling place, one that Jim and I have come to love deeply. It was Don's last work in the world, to pick out this place. As always, he did a fantastic job. It has been a privilege to be able to abide here, where my Donald was alive, where he suffered and died, and where he loved me so well. Jim and I have turned to this lovely little bungalow and its modest yard and have made more and more of it into gardens. We are still working for Don! That gives us both great comfort. Whatever we do, it is only the continuation of that which he so wonderfully began with his sharp mind and wide and thoughtful nature.

It has been a dark-hued experience for me, complete with literally years of suicidal feelings and self-condemnation. Yet, through this catalyst, I have learned to love myself, really to love and care for my self without trying to justify or defend. And this is not so much an advance in loving as it is an advance in wisdom—for one learns to love the mistakes only through wisdom. While I shall definitely never come vaguely close to being as wise as Don, I can feel the gifts he left with me. My intelligence has a persistence and clarity I feel are his gifts to me. And I see it as my remaining personal lesson to follow the pattern of devotion and love through every day and hour of the rest of this earthly life. I live now for both of us, as he died for both of us. And I feel the peace that comes with cooperation with one's destiny.

Session 106 (in total),
March 15, 1984

RA: I am Ra. I greet you in the love and in the light of the One Infinite Creator. We communicate now.

QUESTIONER: Could you first please give me the condition of the instrument?

RA: I am Ra. The parameters of this instrument are marginal, both physically and mental/emotionally. The vital energy of this entity is biased towards strength/weakness.

QUESTIONER: What would the instrument do to make the marginal condition much better?

RA: I am Ra. The instrument is proceeding through a portion of the incarnational experience during which the potential for mortal distortion of the left renal system is great. Less important, but adding to the marginality of distortion towards viability, are severe allergic reactions and the energizing of this and other distortions towards weakness/strength. The mental/emotional complex is engaged in what may best be termed inappropriate compassion.

QUESTIONER: Would Ra recommend the steps which we might take to alleviate or reverse the conditions of which you just spoke?

RA: I am Ra. We can do this. The renal distortions are subject to affirmations. The entity, at present, beginning what may be called initiation, is releasing toxins, and, therefore, larger amounts of liquids to aid in the dilution of these toxins is helpful. The allergies are already being largely controlled by affirmation and the near-constant aid of the healer known as Bob. Further aid may be achieved by the relocation of dwelling and future vigilance against humidity exceeding the healthful amount in the atmosphere breathed.

The mental/emotional distortions are somewhat less easily lessened. However, the questioner and instrument together shall find it possible to do such a working.

QUESTIONER: How serious or critical is this renal problem? Is drinking liquids the only thing she can do for that, or is there something else?

RA: I am Ra. Note the interrelationship of mind and body complexes. This is one example of such interweaving of the design of catalyst and experience. The period of renal delicacy is serious, but only potentially. Should the instrument desire to leave this incarnational experience, the natural and nonenergized opportunity to do so has been in-built, just as the period during which the same entity did, in fact, leave the incarnational experience and then return by choice was inlaid.

However, the desire to leave and be no more a portion of this particular experiential nexus can and has been energized. This is a point for the instrument to ponder and an appropriate point for the support group to be watchful in regards to care for the instrument. So are mind and body plaited up as the tresses of hair of a maiden.

The nature of this entity is gay and sociable, so that it is fed by those things we have mentioned previously: the varieties of experience with other-selves and other locations and events being helpful, as well as the experience of worship and the singing, especially of sacred music. This entity chose to enter a worshipful situation with a martyr's role when first in this geographical location. Therefore, the feeding by worship has taken place only partially. Similarly the musical activities, though enjoyable and therefore of a feeding nature, have not included the aspect of praise to the Creator.

The instrument is in a state of relative hunger for those spiritual homes which it gave up when it felt a call to martyrdom and turned from the planned worship at the location you call the Cathedral of St. Philip. This too shall be healed gradually due to the proposed alteration in location of this group.

QUESTIONER: Then as I understand it, the best thing for us to do is to advise the instrument to drink more liquid. I think water would be best. We will, of course, move. We could move her out of here immediately— tomorrow, say—if necessary. Would this be considerably better than waiting two to three weeks for the allergies and everything else?

RA: I am Ra. Such decisions are a matter for free-will choice. Be aware of the strength of the group harmony.

QUESTIONER: Is there anything, with respect to the present spiritual or metaphysical condition or physical condition of this Hobbs Park Road house, that Ra could tell us about that would be deleterious to the instrument's health?

RA: I am Ra. We may speak to this subject only to note that there are mechanical electrical devices which control humidity. The basement level is one location, the nature of which is much like that which you have experienced at the basement level of your previous domicile. Less humid conditions would remove the opportunity for the growth of those spores to which the instrument has sensitivity. The upper portions of the domicile are almost, in every case, at acceptable levels of humidity.

QUESTIONER: How about the metaphysical quality of the house? Could Ra appraise that, please?

RA: I am Ra. This location is greatly distorted. We find an acceptable description of this location's quality to elude us without recourse to hackneyed words. Forgive our limitations of expression. The domicile and its rear aspect, especially, is blessed, and angelic presences have been invoked for some of your time past.

QUESTIONER: I'm not sure that I understand what Ra means by that. I'm not sure if the place is metaphysically extremely good or extremely negative. Could Ra clear that up, please?

RA: I am Ra. We intended to stress the metaphysical excellence of the proposed location. The emblements of such preparation may well be appreciated by this group.

QUESTIONER: Would the cleansing by salt and water be necessary for this location, then? Or would it be recommended?

RA: I am Ra. There is the recommended metaphysical cleansing as in any relocation. No matter how fine the instrument, the tuning still is recommended between each concert or working.

QUESTIONER: If the instrument stays out of the basement, do you think that the humidity and the physical conditions will be good for the instrument, then? Is that correct?

RA: I am Ra. No.

QUESTIONER: We must do something about the humidity in the whole house, then, to make it good for the instrument. Is that correct?

RA: I am Ra. Yes.

QUESTIONER: I want to come back to a couple of points here, but I want to get in a question about myself. It seems to be critical at this point. Could Ra tell me what is physically wrong with me, what's causing it, and what I could do to alleviate it?

RA: I am Ra. The questioner is one also in the midst of further initiation. During this space/time, the possibility for mental/emotional distortion approaching that which causes the entity to become dysfunctional is marked. Further, the yellow-ray, chemical vehicle of the questioner is aging and has more difficulty in the absorption of needed minerals such as iron and other substances such as papain, potassium, and calcium.

At the same time, the body of yellow ray begins to have more difficulty eliminating trace elements such as aluminum. The energizing effect has occurred in the colon of the questioner, and the distortions in that area are increasingly substantial. Lastly, there is a small area of infection in the mouth of the questioner which needs attention.

QUESTIONER: Could Ra recommend what I should do to improve my state of health?

RA: I am Ra. We tread most close to the Law of Confusion in this instance but feel the appropriateness of speaking due to potentially fatal results for the instrument. We pause to give the questioner and the scribe a few moments of space/time to aid us by stepping away from those distortions which cause us to invoke the Law of Confusion. This would be helpful.

[A few moments' pause]

I am Ra. We appreciate your attempts. Even confusion on your behalves is helpful. The questioner has, in the recent past, allowed a complete transfer of mental/emotional pain from the questioner to the instrument. The key to this deleterious working was when the instrument said words to the effect of the meaning that it would be the questioner and be the strong one. The questioner could be as the instrument, small and foolish. The questioner, in full ignorance of the firm intent of the instrument and not grasping the possibility of any such energy transfer, agreed.

These two entities have been as one for a timeless period and have manifested this in your space/time. Thusly, the deleterious working occurred. By agreement in care and caution, it may be undone. We urge the attention to thanksgiving and harmony on the part of the questioner. We may affirm the previous recommendation in general of the skills and the purity of intention of the one known as Bob, and may note the sympathetic illness which has occurred due to the instrument's sensitivities.

Lastly, we may note that to the one known as Peter, several aspects of the distortions experienced by the questioner, the instrument, and the scribe may be quite apparent and rather simply traduced to lesser distortions.

QUESTIONER: What is Peter's last name? I am not familiar with who he is.

RA: I am Ra. The name by which this entity chooses to be known is Inman.

QUESTIONER: Does Ra think that surgery in my case would be of any help?

RA: I am Ra. We assume you speak of the colonic indisposition and its potential aid by your chirurgeons. Is this correct?

QUESTIONER: Yes.

RA: Again, I am Ra. Please blow across the face and heart of the instrument.

[This was done as directed.]

RA: I am Ra. We shall continue. The atmosphere has been meticulously prepared. However, there are those elements which cause difficulty to the instrument, the neurasthenia of the right side of the face being added to other arthritically energized pain flares.

Such an operation would be of aid in the event that the entity chose this physical cleansing as an event which collaborated with changes in the mental, mental/emotional, and physical orientations of the entity. Without the latter choice, the distortion would recur.

QUESTIONER: Now, going back to summarizing what we can do for the instrument is through praise and thanksgiving. Is that all that we can do, other than advising her to drink a considerable amount of liquid and moving her into a better atmosphere? Am I correct on that?

RA: I am Ra. We examine the statement and find two items missing, one important relative to the other. The chief addition is the grasping of the entity's nature. The less important is, for little it may seem to be, perhaps helpful; that is, the entity absorbs much medication and finds it useful to feed itself when these substances are ingested. The substitution of substances such as fruit juice for the cookie is recommended, and, further, the ingestion of substances containing sucrose which are not liquid is not recommended within four of your hours before the sleeping period.

QUESTIONER: With my experience with the dehumidifiers, I think that it will probably be impossible to lower the humidity in that house much. We can try that, and probably if we do move in there, we will have to move out very shortly.

Is there anything else that needs to be done to complete the healing of Jim's kidney problem?

RA: I am Ra. If it be realized that the condition shall linger in potential for some months after the surcease of all medication, then care will be taken and all will continue well.

We may note that, for the purposes you intend, the location, Hobbs Park Road, whether humid or arid, is uncharacteristically well suited. The aggravated present distortions of the instrument having abated due to lack of acute catalyst, the condition of the location about which the assumption was made is extremely beneficial.

QUESTIONER: Then you are saying that the effect of the humidity—we will try to get it as low as possible—is a relatively minor consideration when all of the other factors of the Hobbs Park Road address are taken into consideration? Is this correct?

RA: I am Ra. Yes.

QUESTIONER: I am quite concerned about the instrument's health at this point. I must ask if there is anything I have failed to consider with respect to the health of the instrument. Is there anything at all that we can do for her to improve her condition other than that which has already been recommended?

RA: I am Ra. All is most wholeheartedly oriented for support here. Perceive the group as here, a location in time/space. Within this true home, keep the light touch. Laugh together and find joy in and with each other. All else is most fully accomplished or planned for accomplishment.

QUESTIONER: Is it as efficacious to cleanse the house with salt and water after we move in as it is before we move in?

RA: I am Ra. In this case it is not an urgent metaphysical concern as timing would be in a less benign and happy atmosphere. One notes the relative simplicity of accomplishing such prior to occupancy. This is unimportant except as regards the catalyst with which you wish to deal.

QUESTIONER: Can you tell me what the instrument's difficulty was with her last whirlpool?

RA: I am Ra. The instrument took on the mental/emotional nature and distortion complex of the questioner, as we have previously noted. The instrument has been taking whirling waters at temperatures which are too hot and at rates of vibration which, when compounded by the heat of the swirling waters, bring about the state of light shock, as you would call the distortion. The mind complex has inadequate oxygen in this distorted state and is weakened.

In this state the instrument, having the questioner's distortion without the questioner's strength of the distortion one might liken to the wearing of armor, began to enter into an acute psychotic episode. When the state of shock was past, the symptoms disappeared. The potential remains as the empathic identity has not been relinquished, and both the questioner and the instrument live as entities in a portion of the mental/emotional complex of the instrument.

May we ask for one more full query at this working and remind the instrument that it is appropriate to reserve some small portion of energy before a working?

QUESTIONER: I would just ask if there is anything that we can do to make the instrument more comfortable or to help her and to improve the contact, and what would be the soonest that Ra would recommend the next contact? I would certainly appreciate the return of the golden hawk. It gave me great comfort.

RA: I am Ra. You have complete freedom to schedule workings.

We suggest the nature of all manifestation to be illusory and functional only insofar as the entity turns from shape and shadow to the One.

I am Ra. We leave you, my friends, in the love and in the glorious light of the One Infinite Creator. Go forth, then, rejoicing in the power and in the peace of the One Infinite Creator. Adonai.

EPILOGUE

After we moved back to Louisville, the mental/emotional dysfunction that Ra spoke of concerning Don occurred. Don was noted all his life for being very cool and extremely wise, emotionally unmoved by events that caused others to fall apart. His observations and advice always proved to be correct. Now, as this dysfunction worsened, Don saw himself intensely affected by even the smallest stimuli. His worrying deepened to depression, and he sought healing counsel from every available source, yet nothing worked, and he resigned himself to a death that he saw quickly approaching.

After seven months of this mental, emotional, and physical deterioration, he became unable to sleep or to eat solid foods. By November he had lost one-third of his body weight and was experiencing intense pain. He refused further hospitalization, which we saw as the last hope for his survival. The thought of having him put into the hospital against his will was abhorrent to us, but we decided to do it and to hope for a miracle, knowing of no other possible way to save Don's life at that point.

When the police came to serve the warrant, a five-and-one-half-hour standoff resulted. Don was convinced his death was imminent, and he did not want to die in a mental hospital. When tear gas was used to bring Don out of the house, he walked out of the back door and shot himself once through the brain. He died instantly.

After his death, Carla saw him three times in waking visions, and he assured us that all was well and that all had occurred appropriately—even if it made no sense at all to us.

So we give praise and thanksgiving for Don's life, for his death, and for our work together.

Though this book is a more personal portion of that work, we hope that you can see that the principles underlying our experiences are the same ones that underlie yours. Though expressions may vary widely, the purpose is the same: that the many portions of the One may know themselves and the One as One. Or, as Ra put it:

"We leave you in appreciation of the circumstance of the great illusion in which you now choose to play the pipe and timbrel and move in rhythm. We are also players upon a stage. The stage changes. The acts ring down. The lights come up once again. And throughout the grand illusion and the following and the following, there is the undergirding majesty of the One Infinite Creator. All is well. Nothing is lost. Go forth rejoicing in the love and the light, the peace, and the power of the One Infinite Creator. I am Ra. Adonai." (from Session 104)

Jim and I have wished to open this personal material for those who feel they might find it useful, because we see in our experiences a good example of the kind of stress that working in the light will produce. The more full of enlightenment the channeling received, the more enlightened the patterns of living and talking need to be. In the case of Don, Jim, and me, all of our outer behavior was correct, and it was not to be held against Don that he didn't become a talker when he got sick. He had never taken another's advice, and he did not want mine or Jim's, then, anymore than usual. And so the tendency Don had of being paranoid bloomed until he was sure I was no longer his love. For him the world without me was unacceptable.

Looking deeper at the timing here, it is crucial that it be seen that I was at this point weighing in at around 84 pounds, at 5 feet, 4 inches. Each session was extremely hard, and yet I never flagged in my desire to continue. I was perfectly willing to die in the process of gaining these sessions' contents. Don was very worried that I would indeed die, and fussed over me continually. There was some mechanism within him that persisted in trying to figure out how to substitute himself for me in taking the brunt of the contact. He spoke about it from time to time, and I always discouraged that line of thinking. But he did just that, in the end. His death ended the contact with those of Ra, and we have never been tempted to take it up again, as we are following Ra's own advice not to do that except with the three of us.

I want to express to each reader the profound feeling of peace that has come to me in the healing of my present incarnation. There will always be that part of me that wishes I could have either been able to save Don or to die with him. I think that is one valid way I could have gone. Then he and I would be a vastly romantic, and quite dead, part of L/L history. But this is not the lesson that was mine. Mine was the lesson concerning wisdom. Ra put it to me quite bluntly when he asked what my time was for going to Jerusalem. He was asking me whether I wanted to martyr myself. This was in the context of questions Don asked concerning the possibility of more-frequent sessions. My response to that was to go on my first vacation in eleven years. Don and I had adventures, NOT vacations!

Don's lesson when our energies and mental distortions were exchanged and merged by our talk in Georgia was concerning the complete opening of his heart. By remaining an observer, he had not yet succeeded in unblocking that great heart of his. In his illness, he truly thought that he was dying that I might be well and live peacefully. There is no more utter devotion and sacrifice than the giving of one's life. It does not matter, in this context, that he was dead wrong. He never lost me, far from it. He lost himself. In his moment of death, he was completely open of heart, and uncaring of the pain of living or of leaving. Of course I have many and conflicting emotions about this. But always I am absolute in my faith that Don's ending was as noble as his life as a whole. To me, he is beyond words. I just adore that soul.

My lesson was the opposite: that of adding wisdom to completely open love. My heart chakra is usually quite unblocked, but my sense of limits has long been shaky. The mind-meld we shared at that time left me with a choice of dying for Don's sake or living for his work, for L/L Research, and all we had done and been together. I did exactly what I had to do to stay in this world. It was touch and go for me for a long time; long after Don's death I was working the energy of death through my own mind, body, and spirit. Through the years, I plumbed the depths of despair, anger (how dare he doubt me!), grief, and sorrow. I faced my own physical death and knew that the crux had come, and the joy of living was still strong within me. This was during the difficult days around Christmas of 1991. I have never been in that much extremity before, not even when my kidneys failed. But my love felt never stronger. I felt as though all was being burned away, and I welcomed that. In the heat of that pain, I felt cleansing and completion. From that time, it was as if a whole new strength had poured into my frail body. As I have achieved a rise from wheelchair and hospital bed, I have felt more and more joy-filled and at the same time transparent. This is a new life I am experiencing, in a new and much replenished body. Indeed, at the age of 54, I feel a grounding and balance that are solid and healthy. I am glad to be here and feel that have entered into the working out of the second pattern that my divided life offers. I bless Don's and my sad tale. And I bless all that has occurred. We loved; we were human. It seems as though we often erred. We did not, for we truly loved. And though I shall always feel orphaned by his absence from my side, I embrace the wonderful things that are now mine to treasure. Jim and I are fueled constantly by the blessing of being able to carry on Don's work.

Any group that stays together and works harmoniously while being of service to the light will begin to attract psychic greeting of the sorts we experienced. In this crucible, every fault and vanity, however small, is a weapon against the self. Ethical perception needs to remain very alert and cogent of issues and values being tossed around. This is a matter of life and death. L/L Research is a special and wonderful place, and not unlike many other lighthouses other wanderers and seekers have lit. Many, many others are awakening now and wishing to become ever more able to be channels for light. And it is a wondrous ministry, to be there as a metaphysical or spiritual home for wanderers and outsiders everywhere. We hope this helps you and your group to stay in full communication, to refuse to offer each other less than joy and faith, no matter what! And never, NEVER to make a deal with the loyal opposition!

We at L/L Research continue to keep our doors open for regular meetings, and many visitors come through our doors, through the snail mail and email, and as our books continue to be spread around, those who are aware of Ra's ideas are all over the globe. Our email address is contact@llresearch.org, our website is www.llresearch.org, and our snail-mail address is L/L Research, PO Box 5195, Louisville, Kentucky 40255-5195. We answer each piece of mail and are always glad to hear from readers old and new. Our hearts are eternally grateful for each other, for Don, for those of Ra and the contact they shared with us. Blessings to all who read this book.

L/L Research
Carla L. Rueckert
Jim McCarty

Louisville, Kentucky
December 20, 1997

ENDNOTES

1. puissance: The power to accomplish or achieve; potency [< OF]
2. sigil: A seal or signet; a mark or sign supposed to exercise occult power. [< L *siggilum* seal]
3. chary: Cautious, careful, wary; fastidious; particular; sparing, frugal; stingy [<OE *cearig* sorrowful, sad < *cearu* care]
4. contumely: Insulting rudeness in speech or manner; scornful insolence; an insult, or an insulting act [<OF *contumelie* < L *contumelia* reproach]
5. demesne: In feudal law, lands held in one's own power; a manor house and the adjoining lands in the immediate use and occupation of the owner of the estate; the grounds belonging to any residence, or any landed estate; any region over which sovereignty is exercised; domain. [< AF *demeyne, OF demeine, demaine. Doublet of domain.*]

INDEX

A
Abductions, ufo, 22
Aging, 179, 187
Allergy, 116, 134–135, 141
Allison, Lawrence, 95
Anger, 78, 83, 91–92, 130, 136–139, 141, 144, 149, 171, 178, 195

B
Balancing, 42, 54, 79, 91–92, 96, 113–114, 138, 142, 166, 183
Ball lightning, 88
Banishing ritual of the lesser pentagram, 108, 110
Battle Beyond the Stars, 47

C
Catalyst, 9–10, 14, 25, 40, 52, 57, 100, 113, 125–129, 131, 139–140, 143, 146–149, 161–162, 167–168, 177, 184–185, 190
Cats, our, 81–82, 131, 136, 164
Cayce, Edgar, 52, 62
Celibacy, 37, 67, 72
Challenging a contact, 12–13
Channeling, 11–14, 28, 44, 51–52, 66, 72, 75, 86, 98, 109, 131–132, 194
Christianity, 60
Church of Christ Scientist, 94
Cleansing ritual, 146
Conditioning vibration, 11
Confederation of planets in the service of the infinite creator, 14
Conspiracy theories, 17–18

INDEX

Cosmic awareness communications, 54
Cosmic mind, 45
Crowley, Aleister, 35–36, 41
Crucifixion of Esmerelda Sweetwater, 28, 102–104
Crystals, 117

D
Deleterious energy exchange, 143, 180–184, 188, 190–191
Devotional life, 27, 40, 95

E
Earth changes, 12–13, 99, 114–115
Einstein, Albert, 34
Eisenhower at Edwards Air Force Base, 47–48
Elkins, Don, 9–10
Exercise, 14, 51, 54, 57–58, 68, 97, 100–101, 103, 112, 114, 116, 125, 142–143, 162–163, 165–166, 181–182, 197

F
Faults, 91
Food, 28, 94, 99, 156, 164
Forgetting process, 26, 59–60
Fortune, Dion, 49
Free will, 11, 18, 26, 30–31, 43, 45, 49–50, 57–58, 66, 88, 90–91, 98, 103, 106, 114, 116, 118, 122, 125, 127–130, 136, 139, 163, 170, 177
Frontal lobes, (of the brain), 85–87
Frye, Daniel, 24

G
Global mind, 27
Golden Dawn, 70
Guides, personal, 33, 60, 87–88

H
Hangar, 47
Harmony, 9, 13, 15–16, 26, 36–37, 60, 66–67, 101, 122, 138, 142, 145, 151, 162, 166, 175, 180, 186, 188
Harvest, 19, 21
Healing, 25, 30, 39, 41–44, 53–54, 72, 93–94, 108, 112, 136, 141, 143–144, 152–153, 158, 175, 179, 189, 193–194
Higher self, 59–61, 76, 96, 128–129, 146, 148–149

Hobbs Park Road Hhouse, 186
Holy Spirit, 60

I
Illness, 50, 94, 98, 131, 146, 149, 153, 159, 164, 171, 175, 179, 183, 188, 195
Impatience, 79, 112, 114
Initiation, 69–70, 121, 181, 185, 187

J
Judgment, 36, 68, 73, 96, 99, 122, 132, 150

K
Karma, 25

L
Law of Confusion, (*see* free–will Law of Responsibility)
L/L Research, 16, 37, 47, 52, 102, 131, 146, 182, 195–196, 204
Love, 14–15, 17–19, 27, 31, 33, 38–40, 49–50, 54, 57, 59–60, 62, 67, 73, 75–77, 79, 81, 84, 89–91, 94, 97, 100, 102, 105, 107–110, 113–115, 119, 130–132, 138–139, 142, 146–147, 150–154, 156, 158, 160–161, 164–165, 170–171, 173–174, 180, 182, 184, 191, 194–195
LSD, 35–36, 41–42, 50–51, 66

M
Marijuana, 36, 42
Martyrdom, 72–73, 92, 118, 142–143, 162, 166, 174, 186
Meditation, 13, 16, 26, 29, 32–33, 43, 47, 51–52, 58, 60, 69–70, 76, 82–83, 93–95, 97, 109, 117, 133, 140, 148
Men in Black, 26, 29
Mind link, 19, 28, 58
Mixed contacts, 12, 47

N
Noyes rhythm foundation, 163

O
Oahspe, 62
Original thought, the, 15
Orion group, 22, 48, 50, 82, 92

Oversoul, 59, 61

P
Polarization, 53, 77, 143, 146, 148, 177
Positive contacts, 90
Prayer of St. Francis, 43
Pre-incarnative choices, 85
Psychic greeting, 25, 49, 67, 72, 132, 143, 151, 174, 195
Psychic sensitivity, 74–75, 80
Puharich, Andrija, 19, 27–29, 42–43, 46, 58, 89, 114–116
Pyramids, 52–53

Q
Q'uo, 33

R
Ra contact, nature of, 9–13, 16–17, 19, 26, 32–33, 64, 66, 71–77, 92–93, 105–108, 118–122, 137, 145–146
Reincarnation, 163, 170

S
Self-acceptance, 113–114
Service, 9, 12, 14–15, 19, 26–27, 30, 32, 34–35, 40, 42, 44–45, 50, 52–53, 56–57, 59–60, 62, 64–66, 68, 70–71, 73–75, 77, 80, 83, 92–96, 98–99, 102–103, 105–106, 108–109, 117–119, 121–122, 125, 128–130, 133, 142–143, 146, 149, 159, 161, 177, 195
Sexual energy transfer, 35–36, 42, 50, 83–85
Shockley, Paul, 52
Signals, personal signs, 89, 124, 128–130, 177
Silver flecks, 31–32, 89–90
Social memory complex, 19, 22, 45, 52–53, 59, 61, 80–81, 134, 177
Spiritual gifts, 79, 121
Spiritual listening, 53–54
Spontaneous combustion, human, 32, 34
Sprinkle, Leo, 88–89

T
Telepathy, 13
Tesla, Nikola, 20–21
Transient information, 18, 99
Tree of life, 77

Tunguska, 32–33
Tuning, 12–13, 32, 43–44, 86, 97, 165, 187

U
Ufos, 17, 28, 47, 64–65, 86

W
Wanderers, 10, 26–28, 30–31, 45–46, 58–59, 63, 79–80, 130, 195–196
Weapons, particle–beam, 21, 34, 100
Williamson, George Hunt, 28
Wisdom, 28, 40, 71, 81, 84, 92, 96–97, 103, 132, 139, 142, 144, 146–147, 182–184, 194–195

ABOUT THE AUTHORS

DON ELKINS was born in Louisville, Kentucky, in 1930. He held a BS and MS in mechanical engineering from the University of Louisville, as well as an MS in general engineering from Speed Scientific School. He was professor of physics and engineering at the University of Louisville for twelve years from 1953 to 1965. In 1965 he left his tenured position and became a Boeing 727 pilot for a major airline to devote himself more fully to UFO and paranormal research. He also served with distinction in the US Army as a master sergeant during the Korean War.

Don Elkins began his research into the paranormal in 1955. In 1962, Don started an experiment in channeling, using the protocols he had learned from a contactee group in Detroit, Michigan. That experiment blossomed into a channeling practice that led eventually to the Law of One material 19 years later. Don passed away on November 7, 1984.

CARLA L. RUECKERT (McCarty) was born in 1943 in Lake Forest, Illinois. She completed undergraduate studies in English literature at the University of Louisville in 1966 and earned her master's degree in library service in 1971.

Carla became partners with Don in 1968. In 1970, they formed L/L Research. In 1974, she began channeling and continued in that effort until she was stopped in 2011 by a spinal fusion surgery. During four of those thirty-seven years of channeling (1981–1984), Carla served as the instrument for the Law of One material.

In 1987, she married Jim McCarty, and together they continued the mission of L/L Research. Carla passed into larger life on April 1, 2015.

JAMES MCCARTY was born in 1947 in Kearney, Nebraska. After receiving an undergraduate degrees from the University of Nebraska at Kearney and a master of science in early childhood education from the University of Florida, Jim moved to a piece of wilderness in Marion County, Kentucky, in 1974 to build his own log cabin in the woods, and to develop a self-sufficient lifestyle. For the next six years, he was in almost complete retreat.

He founded the Rock Creek Research and Development Laboratories in 1977 to further his teaching efforts. After experimenting, Jim decided that he preferred the methods and directions he had found in studying with L/L Research in 1978. In 1980, he joined his research with Don's and Carla's.

Jim and Carla were married in 1987. Jim has a wide L/L correspondence and creates wonderful gardens and stonework. He enjoys beauty, nature, dance, and silence.

NOTE: The Ra contact continued until session number 106. There are five volumes total in The Law of One series, Book I–Book V. There is also other material available from our research group on our archive website, www.llresearch.org.

You may reach us by email at contact@llresearch.org, or by mail at: L/L Research, P.O. Box 5195, Louisville, KY 40255-0195

Notes

Notes

Notes

Notes